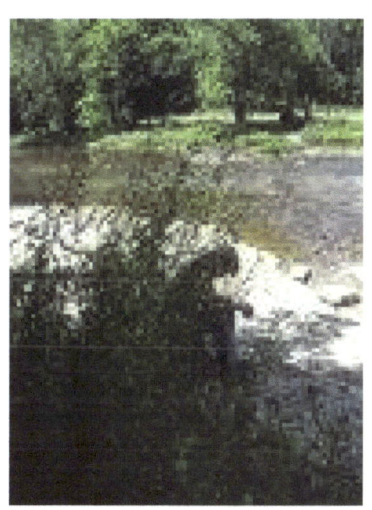

THE BEAUTY OF A PICTURE

This book contains pictures that are very dear to my heart. My hope is that you enjoy each picture as much as I do.

I would like to dedicate this book to my Dad. He taught me to appreciate the beauty in the smallest of things. I love you Dad, and I am sure the view from Heaven is amazing!

A Collection of Some Of My Favorite Photography

By

Barbara E. Young

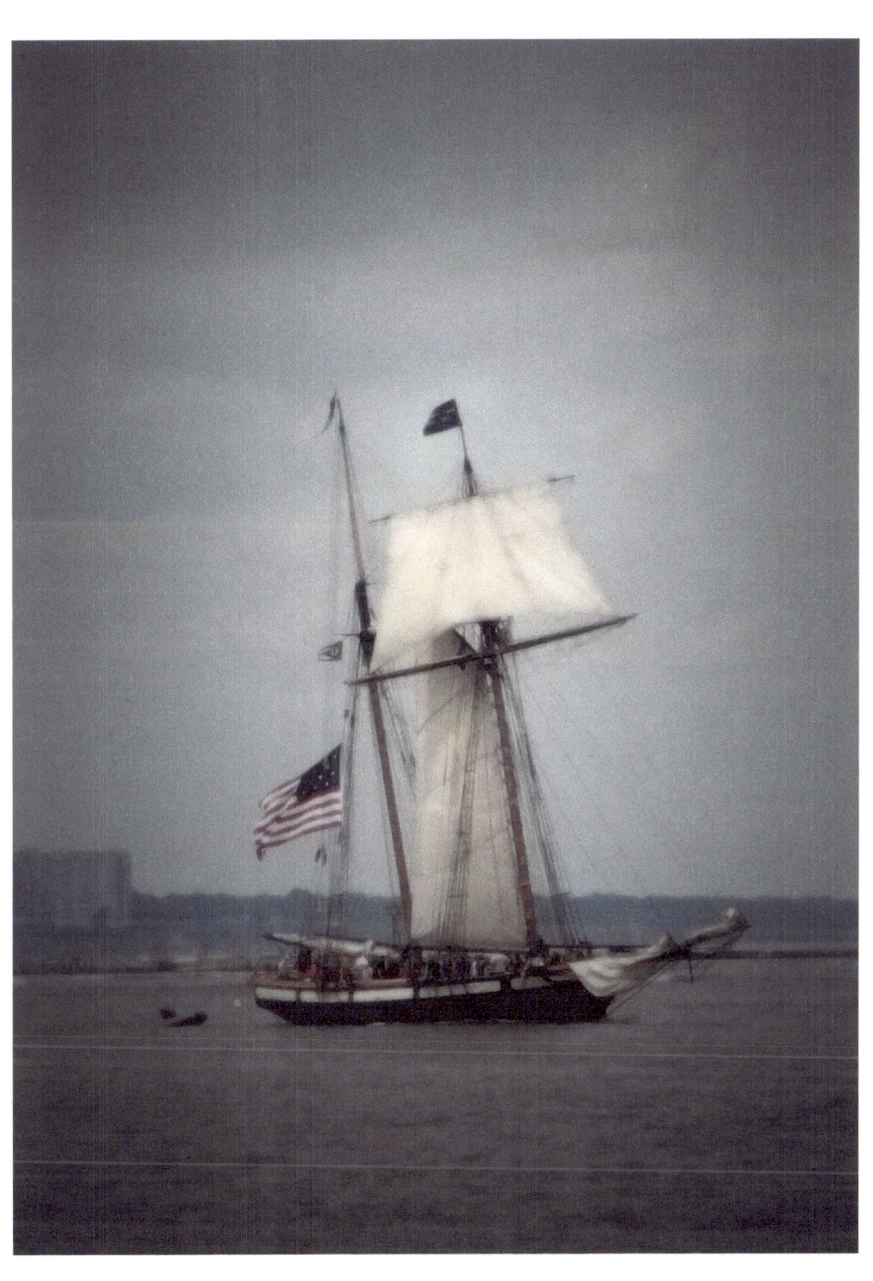

-Beauty, on the waters of Lake Erie-

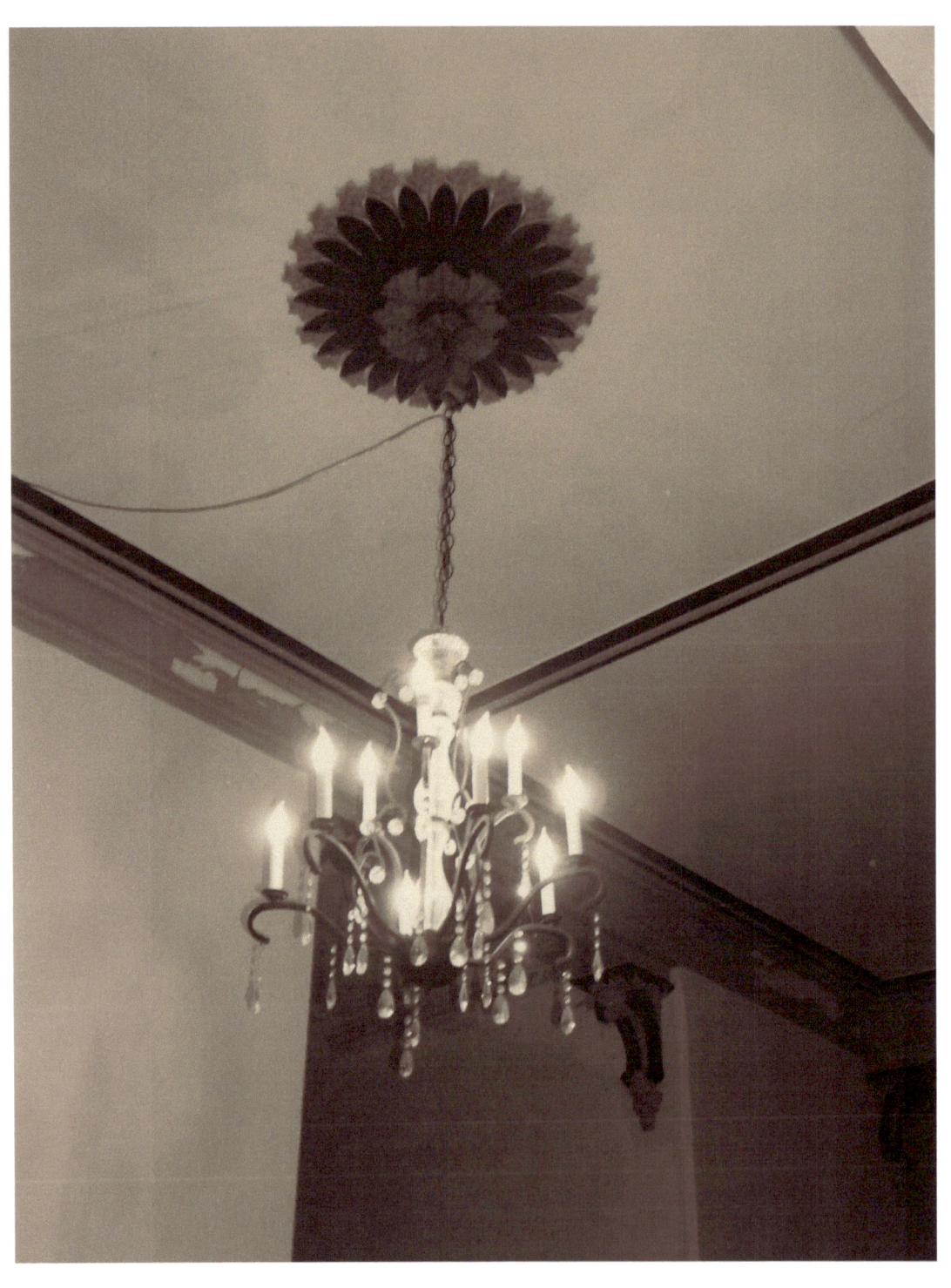

-Light the Way-

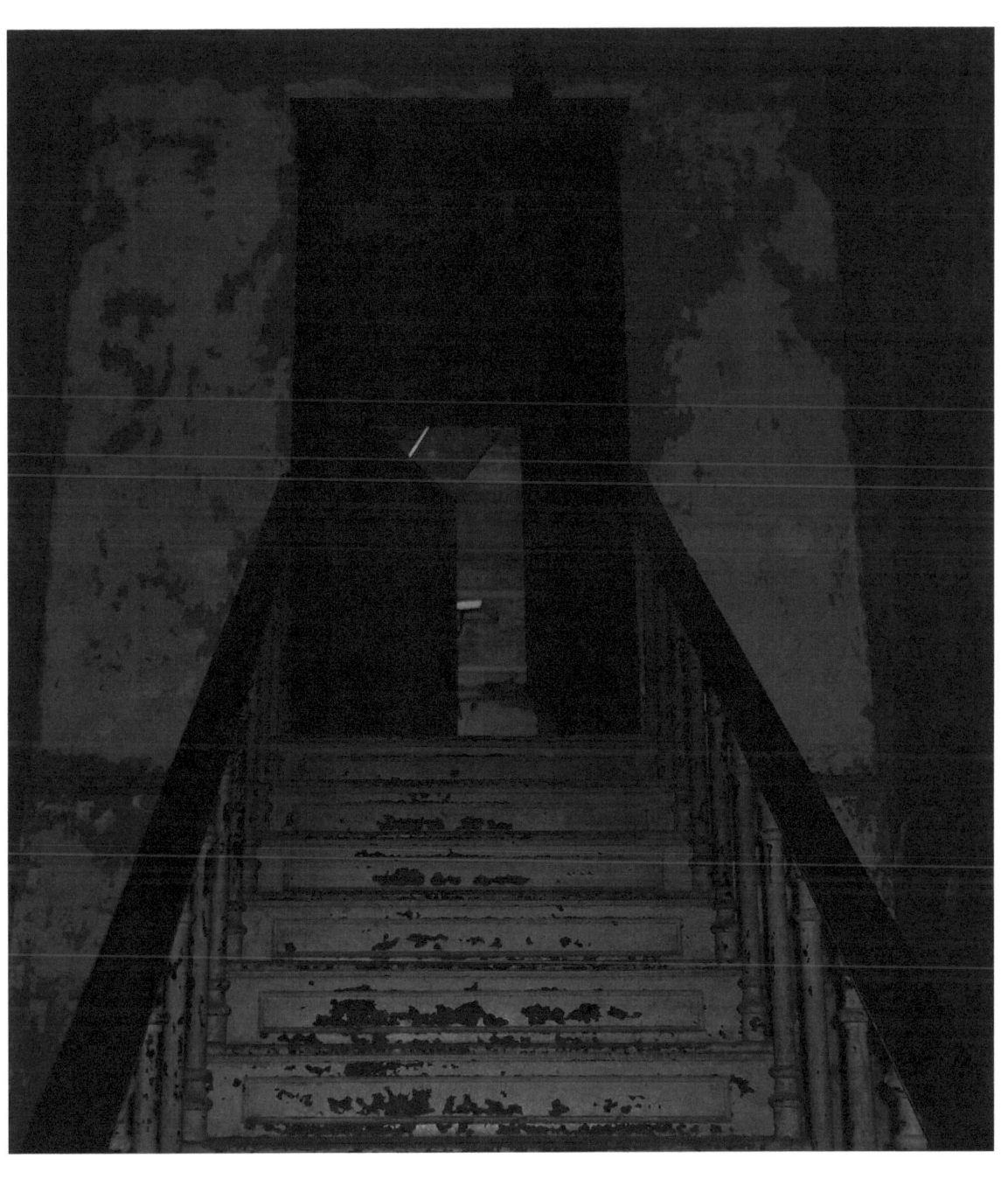

- Come on in, we have been expecting you -

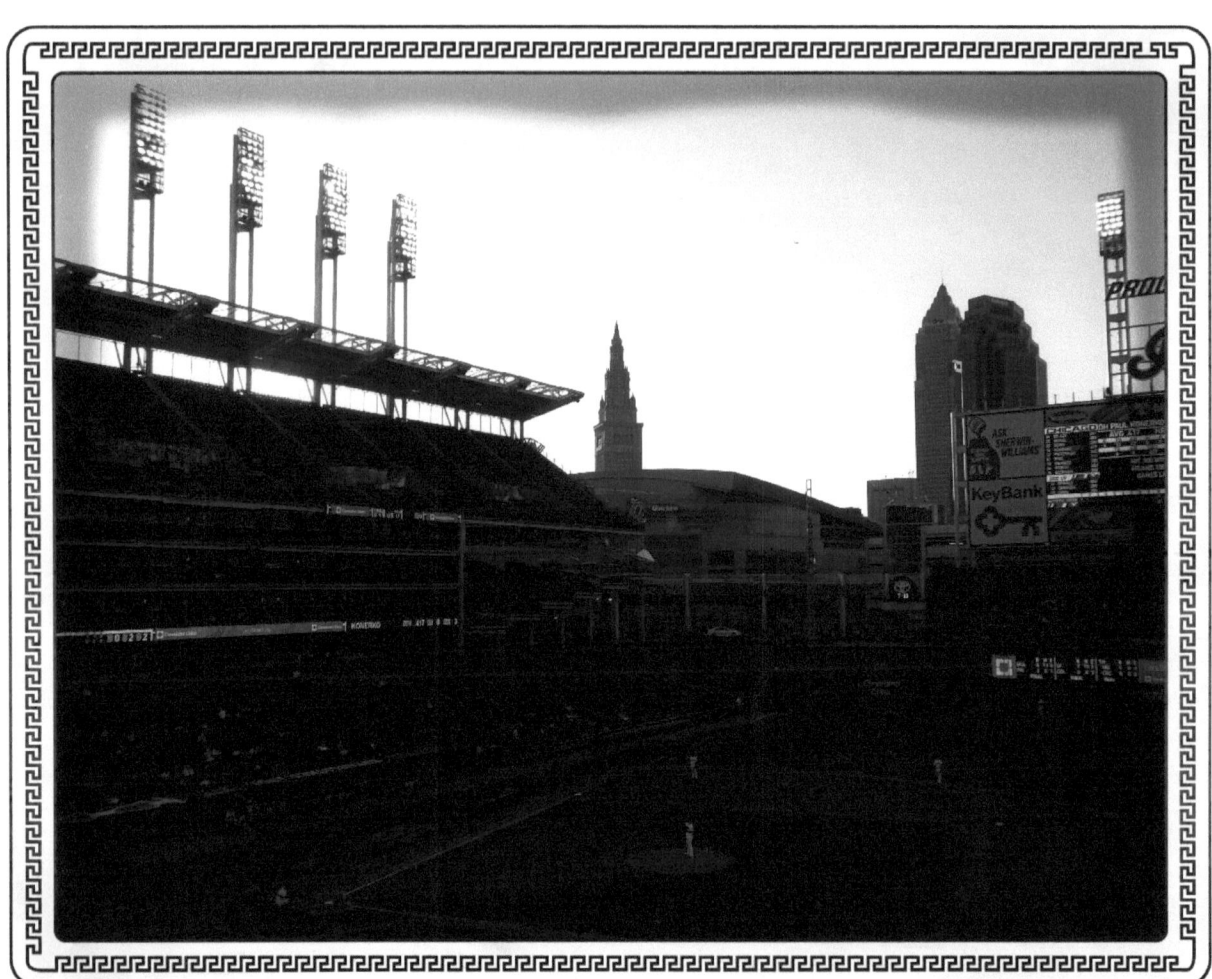

-A Great Day for a Game-

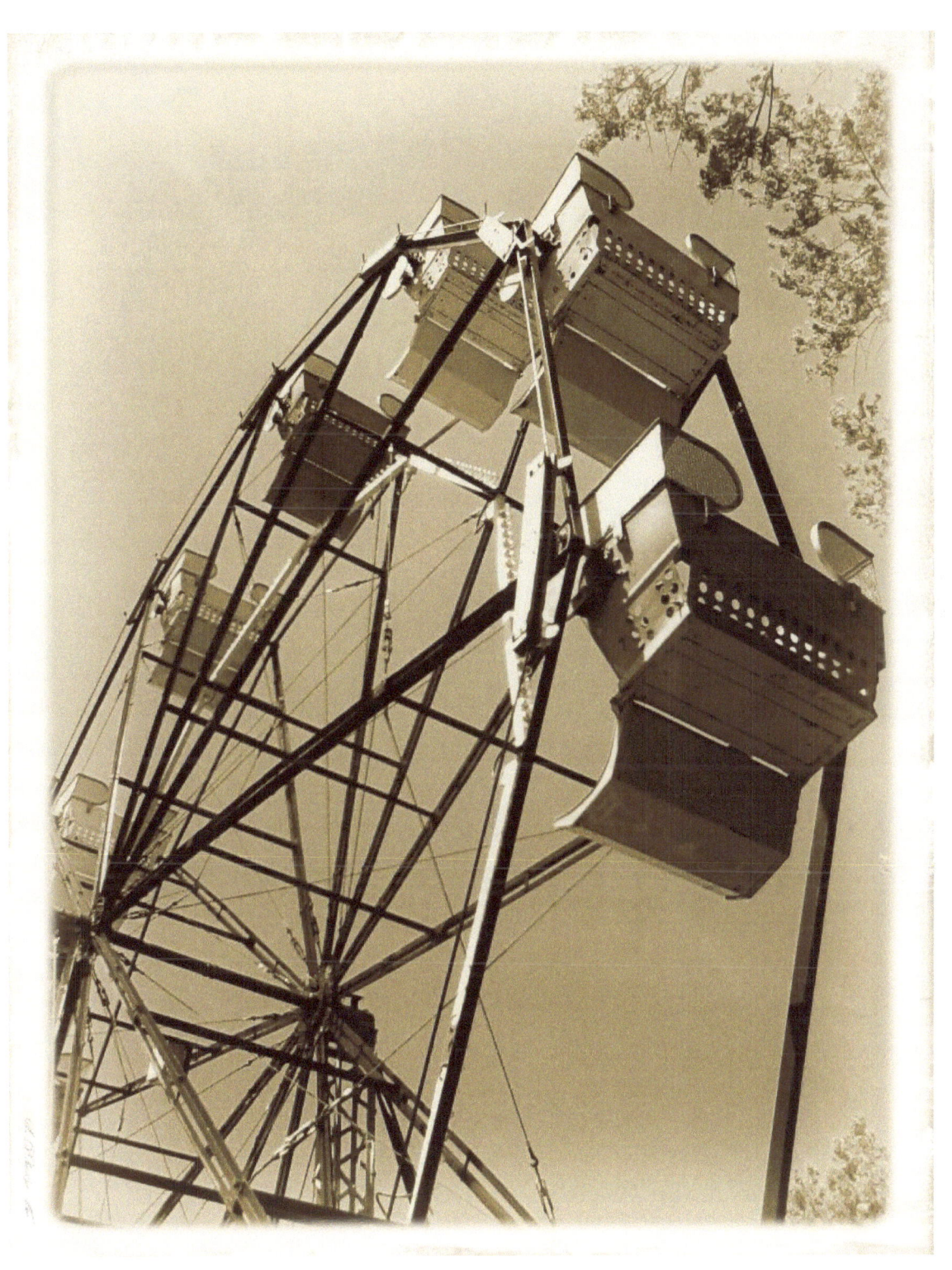

-Let's Take a Ride-

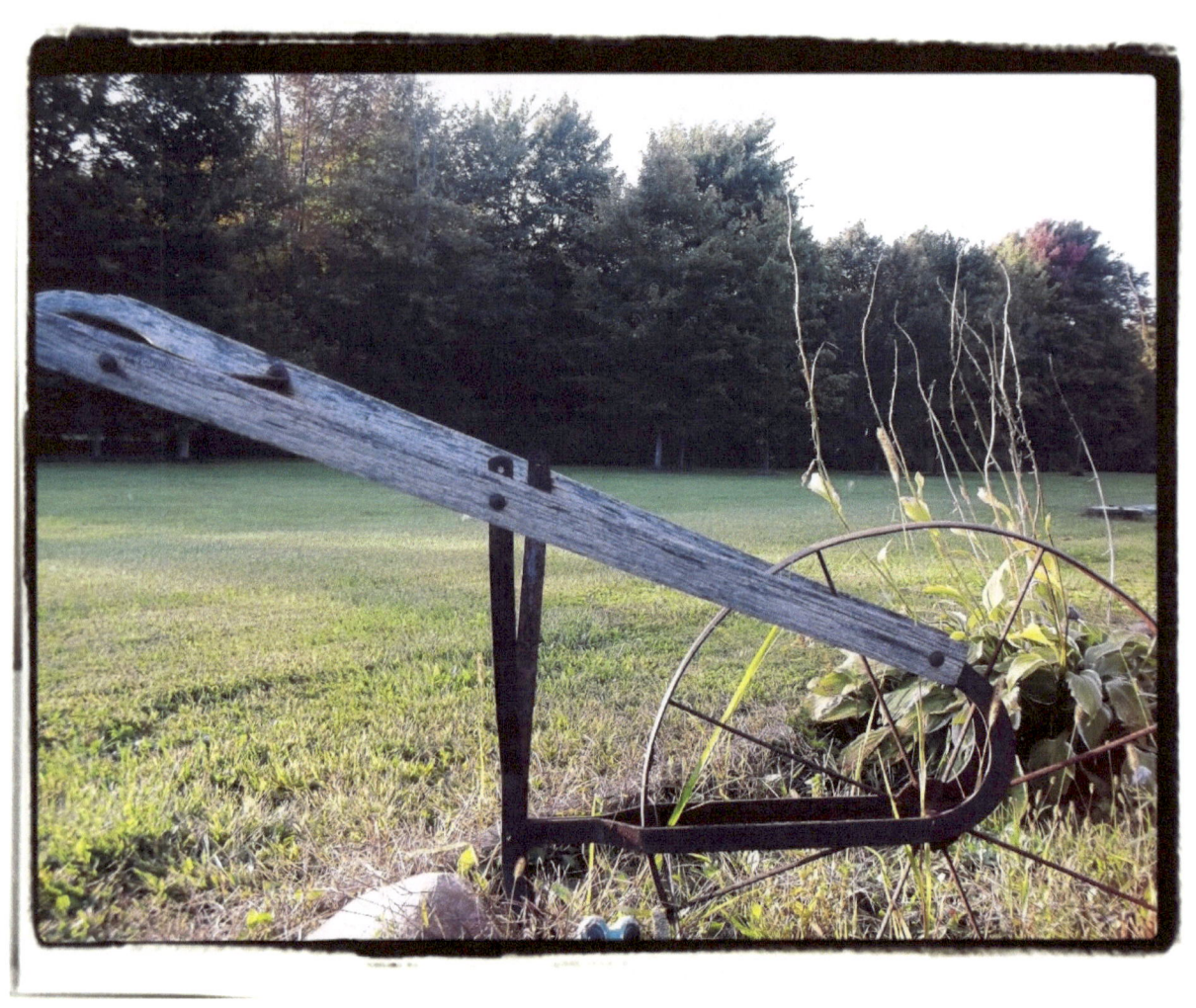

-The Beginning of Fall-

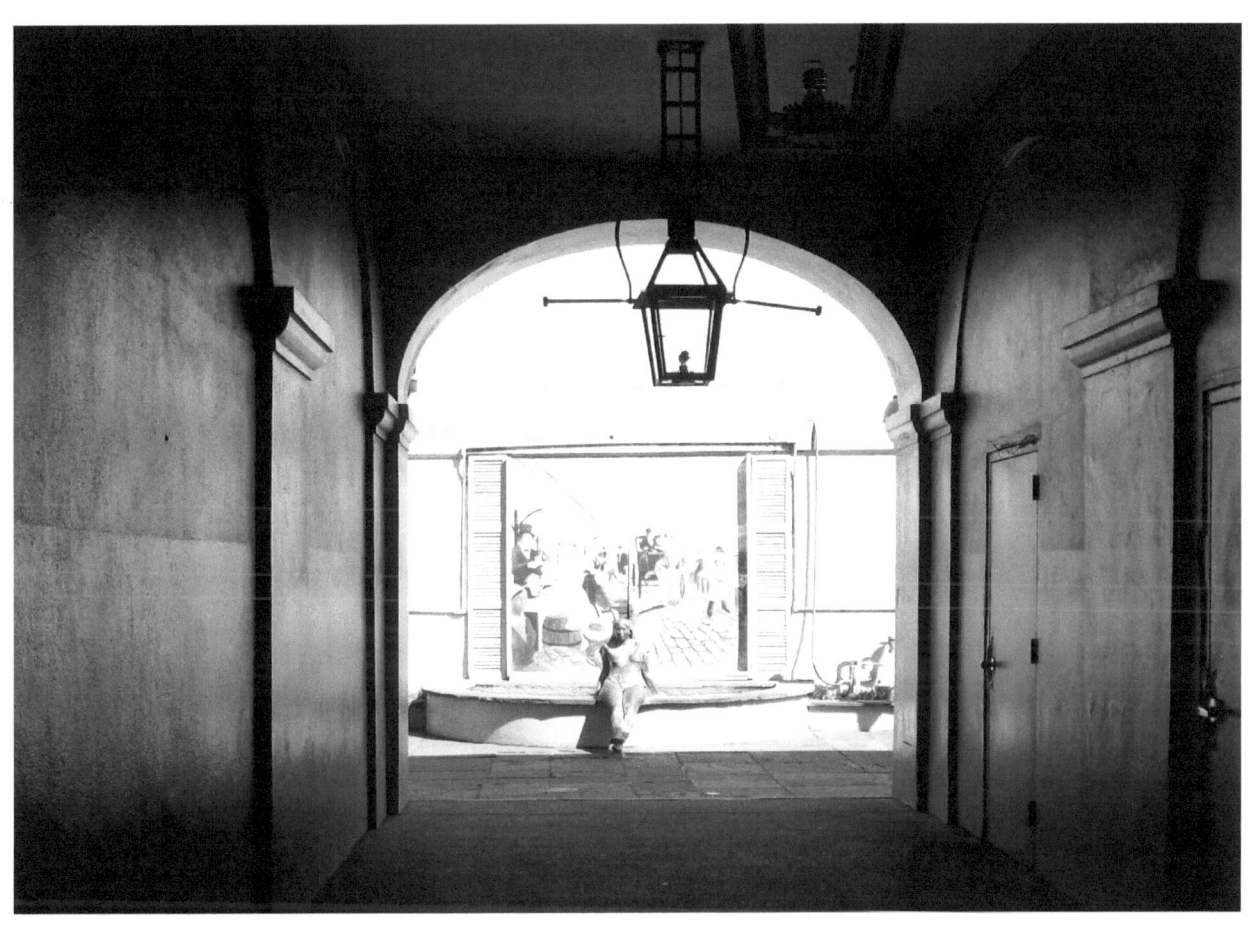

-*A Moment of Quiet Meditation*-

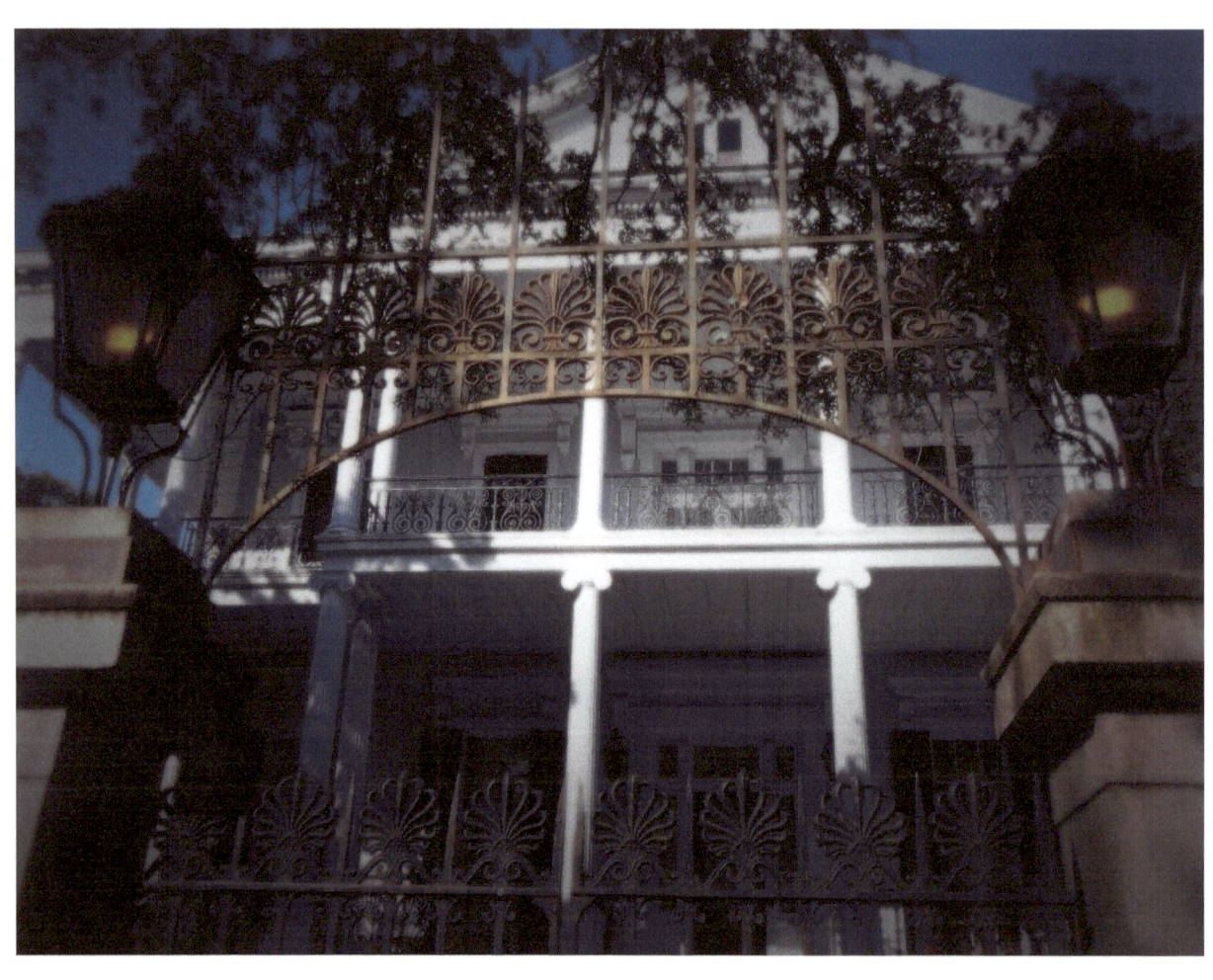

-If only these Walls could Talk-

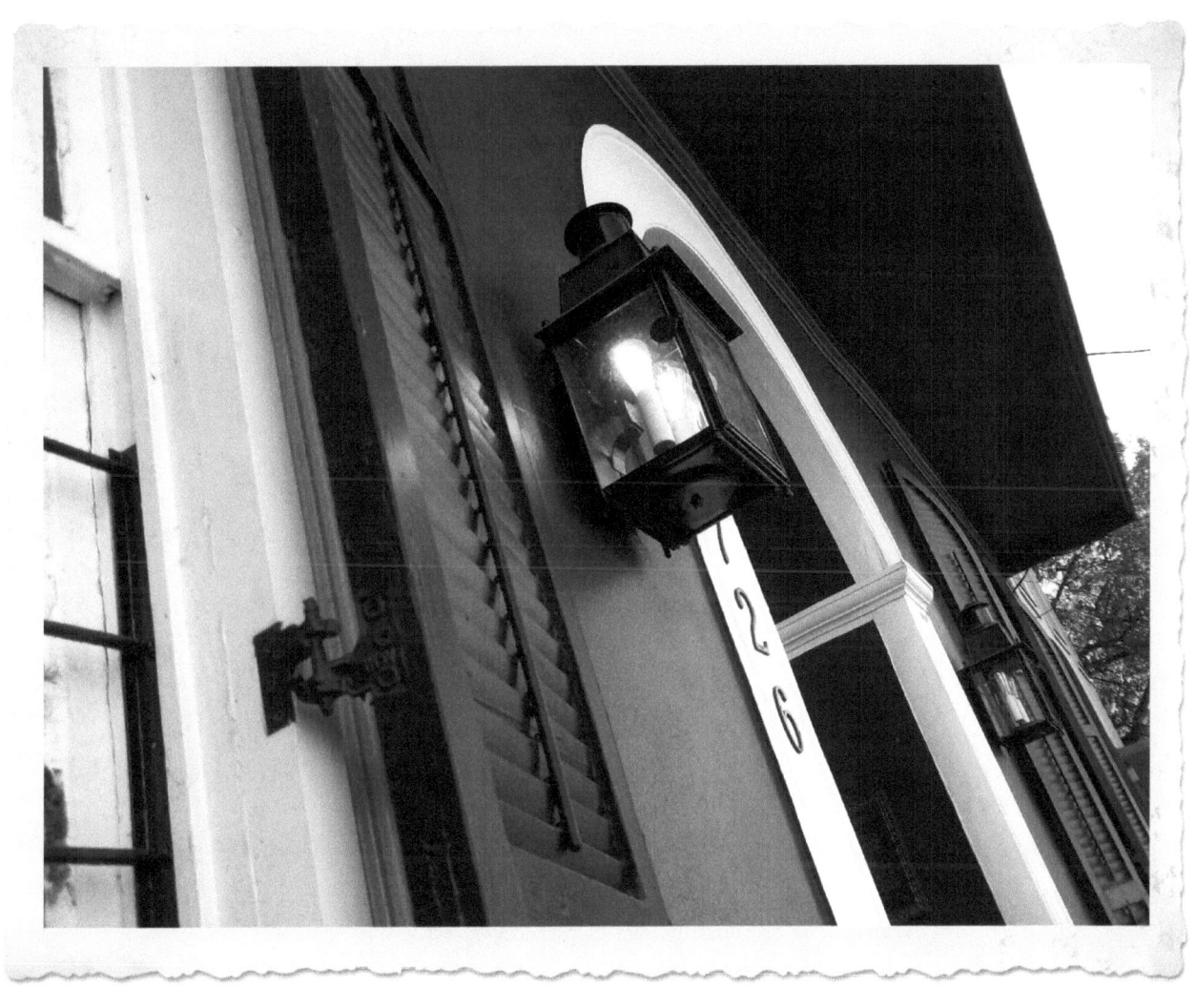

-Light up my path-

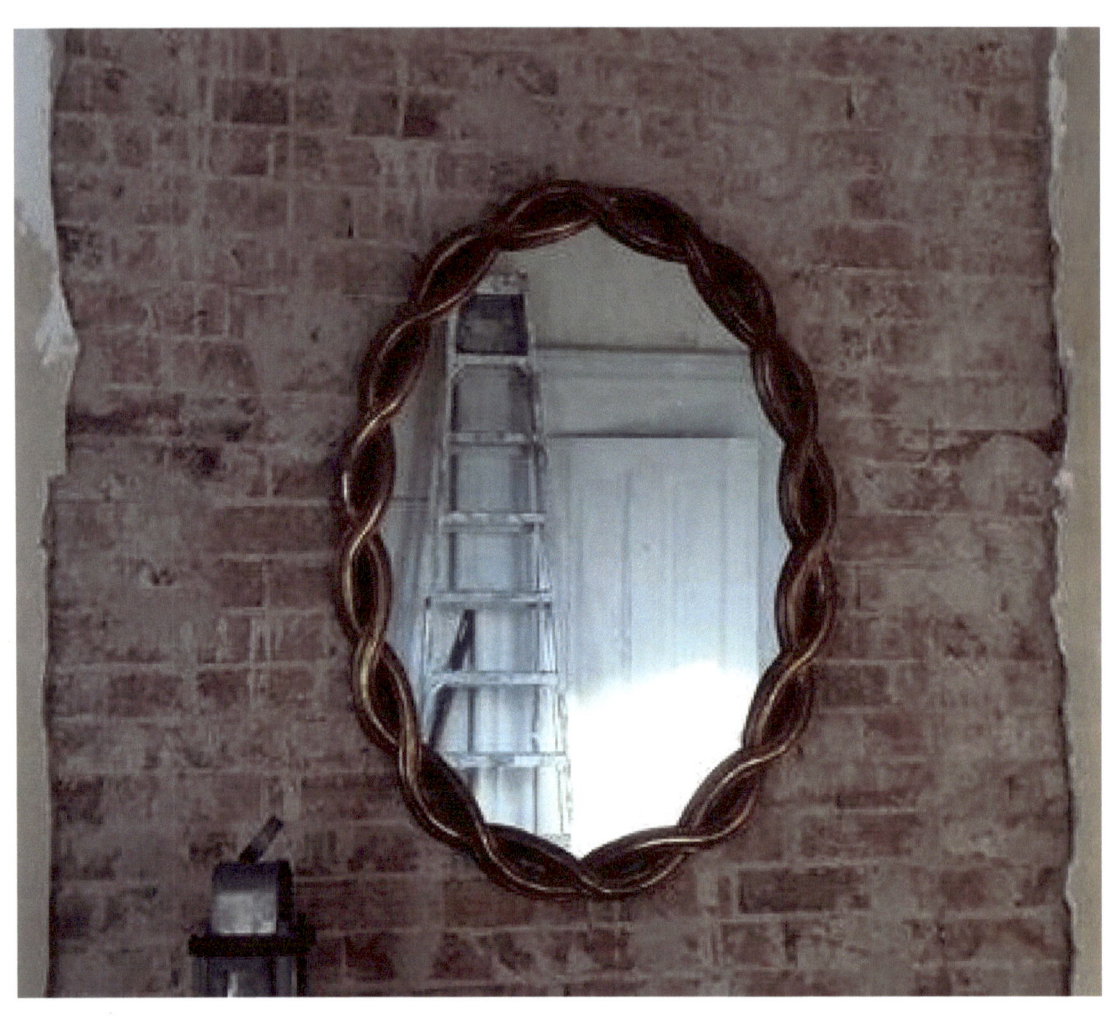

-We are all a work in progress-

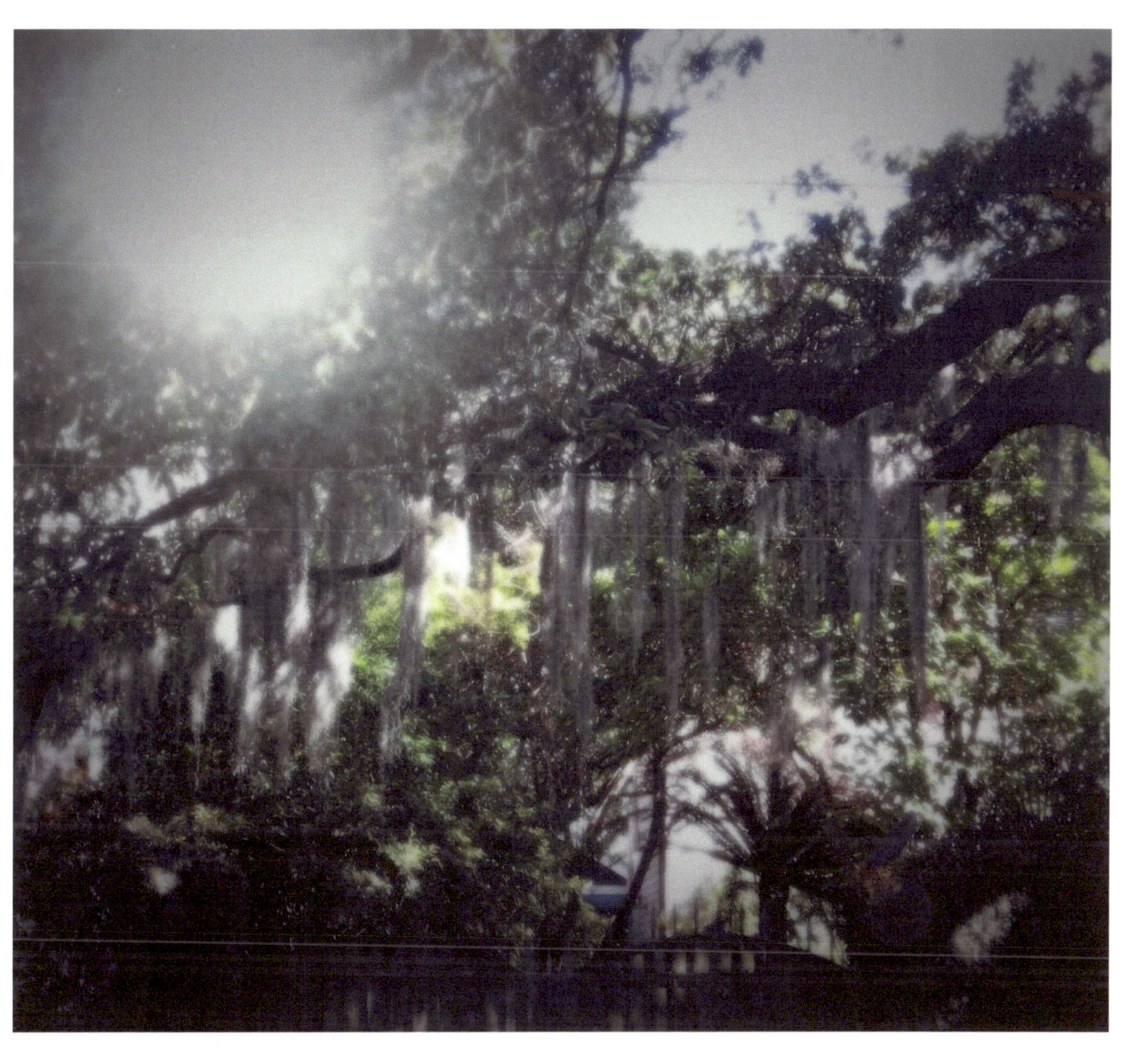

-*A Stroll in New Orleans*-

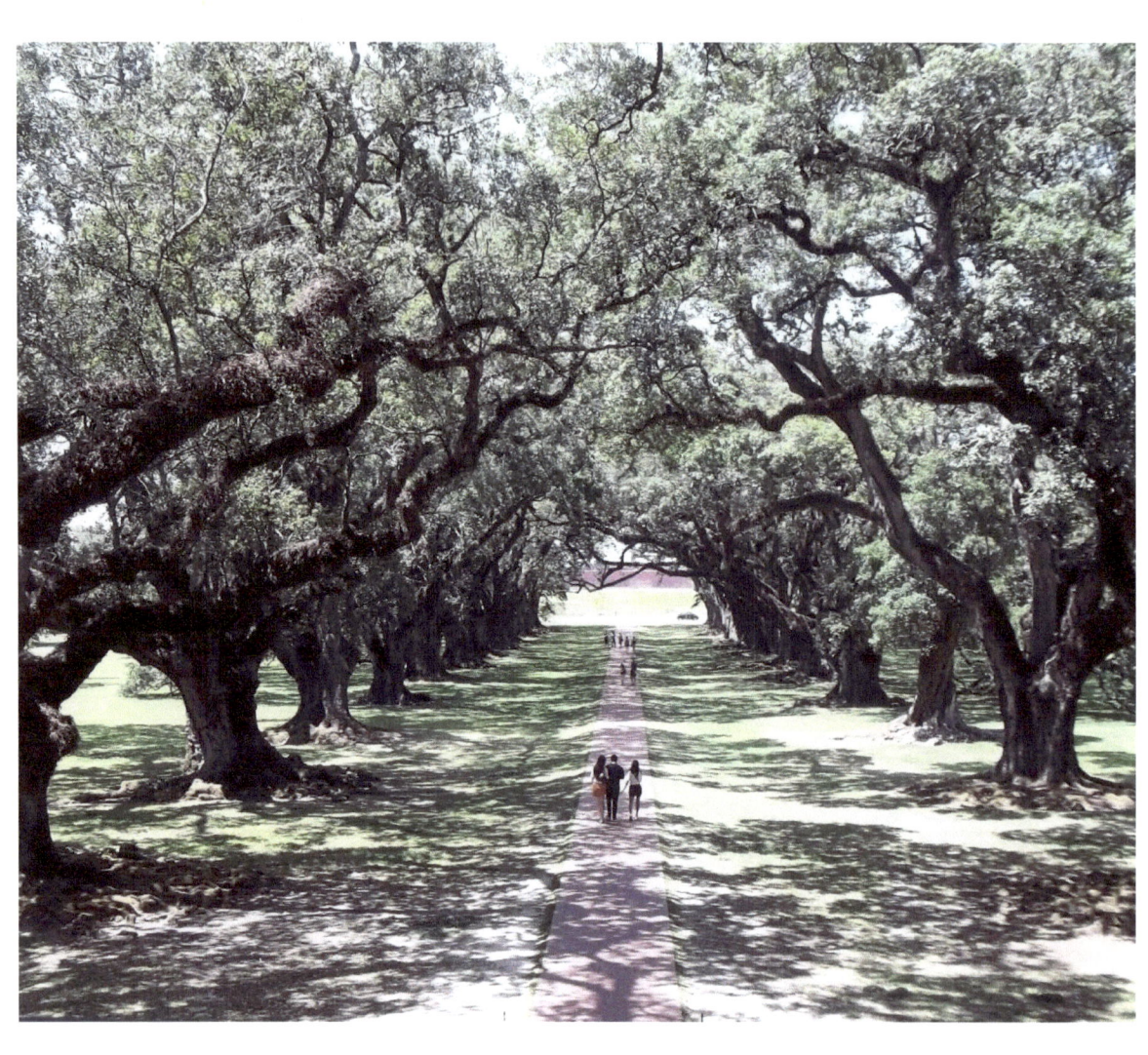

-Walk with Me-

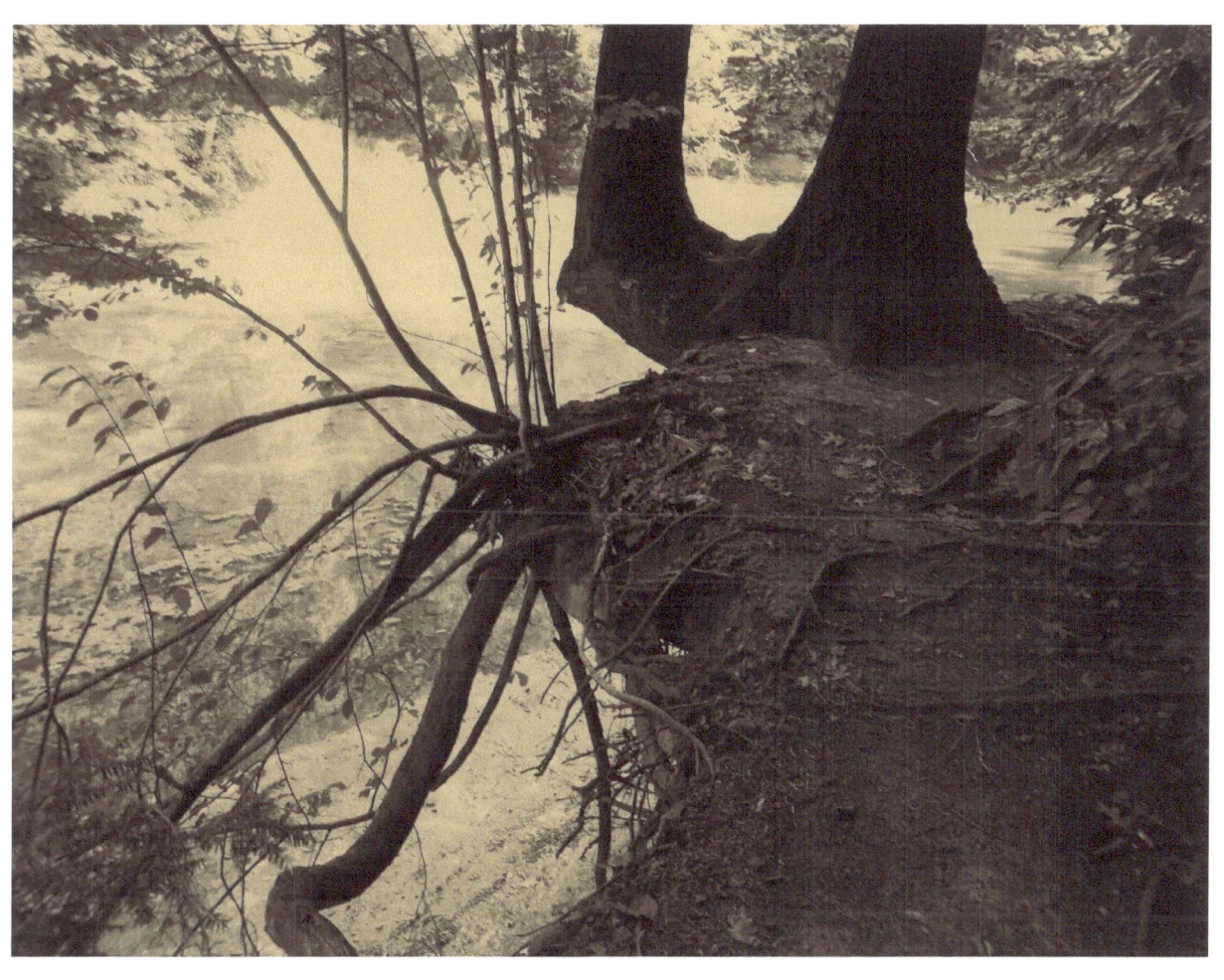

-Lay Down Some Roots-

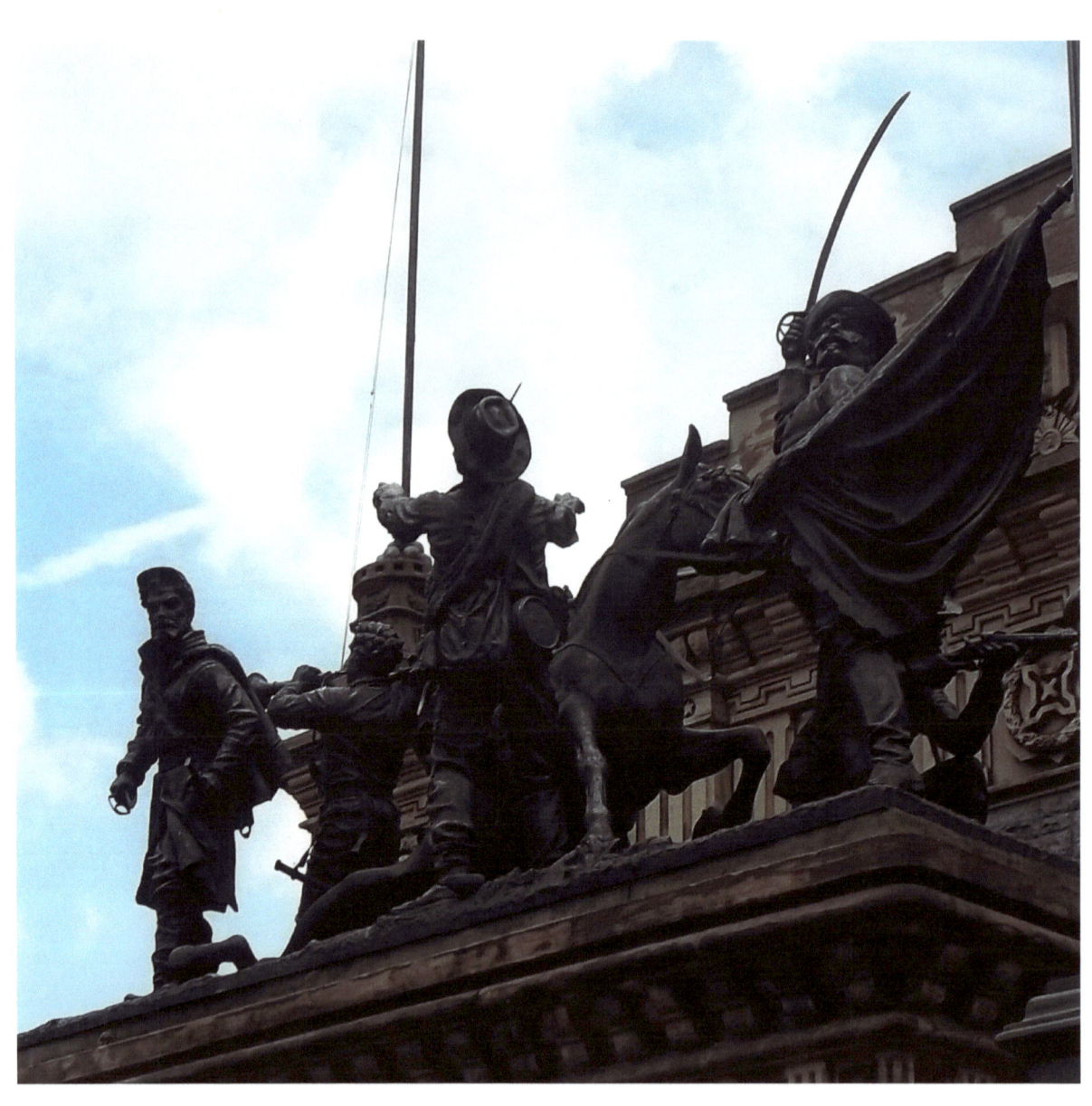

-The Few, The Brave-

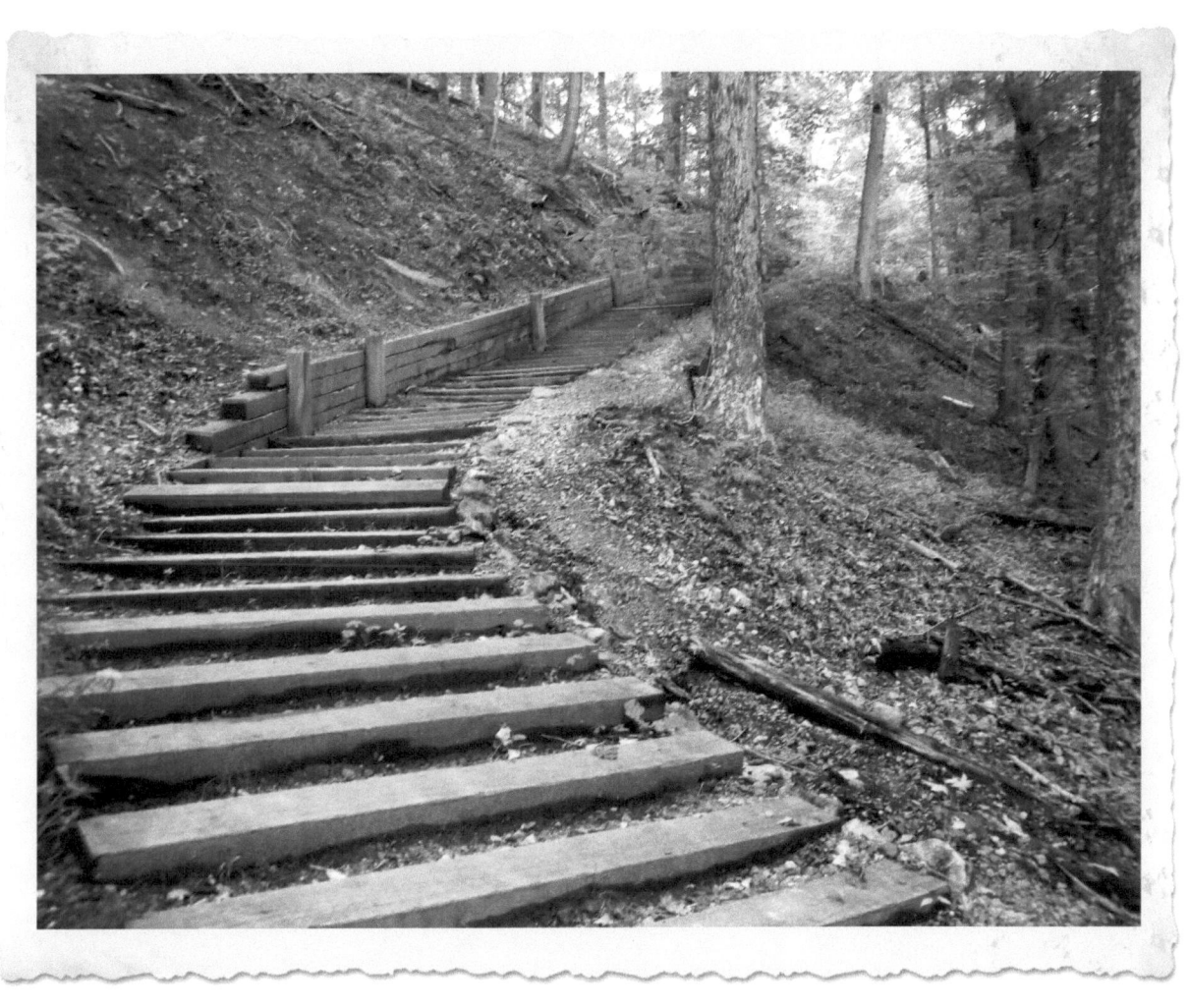

-Stairway to Tranquility-

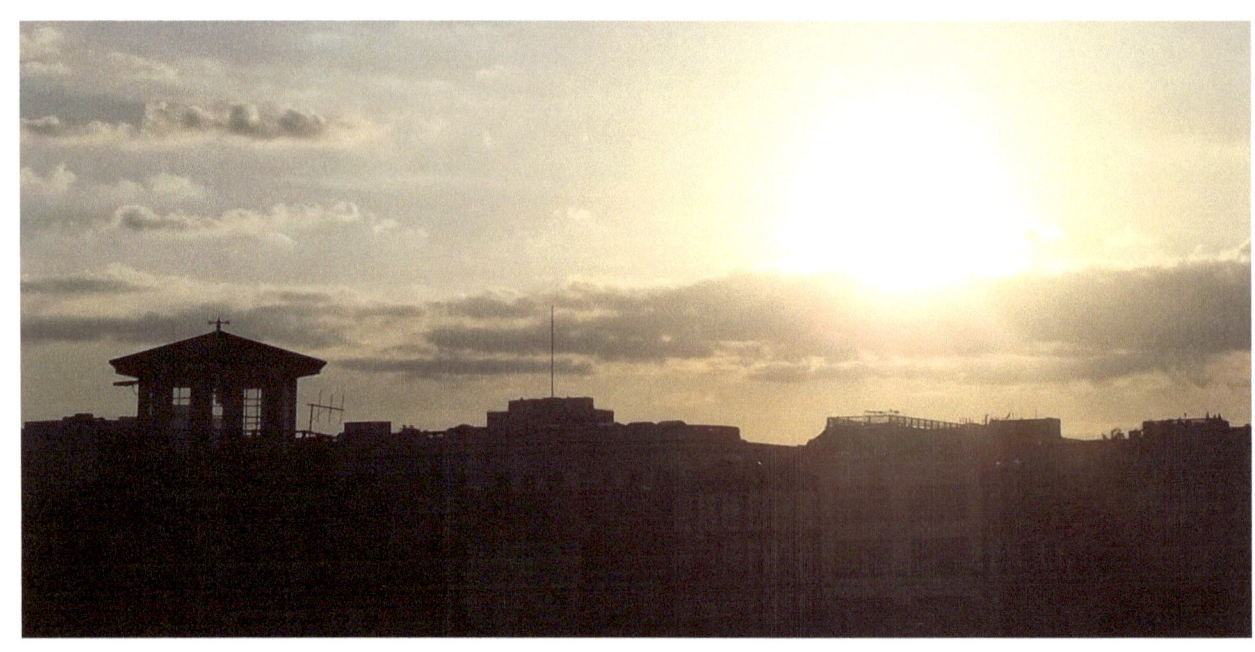

-Sunset in the French Quarter-

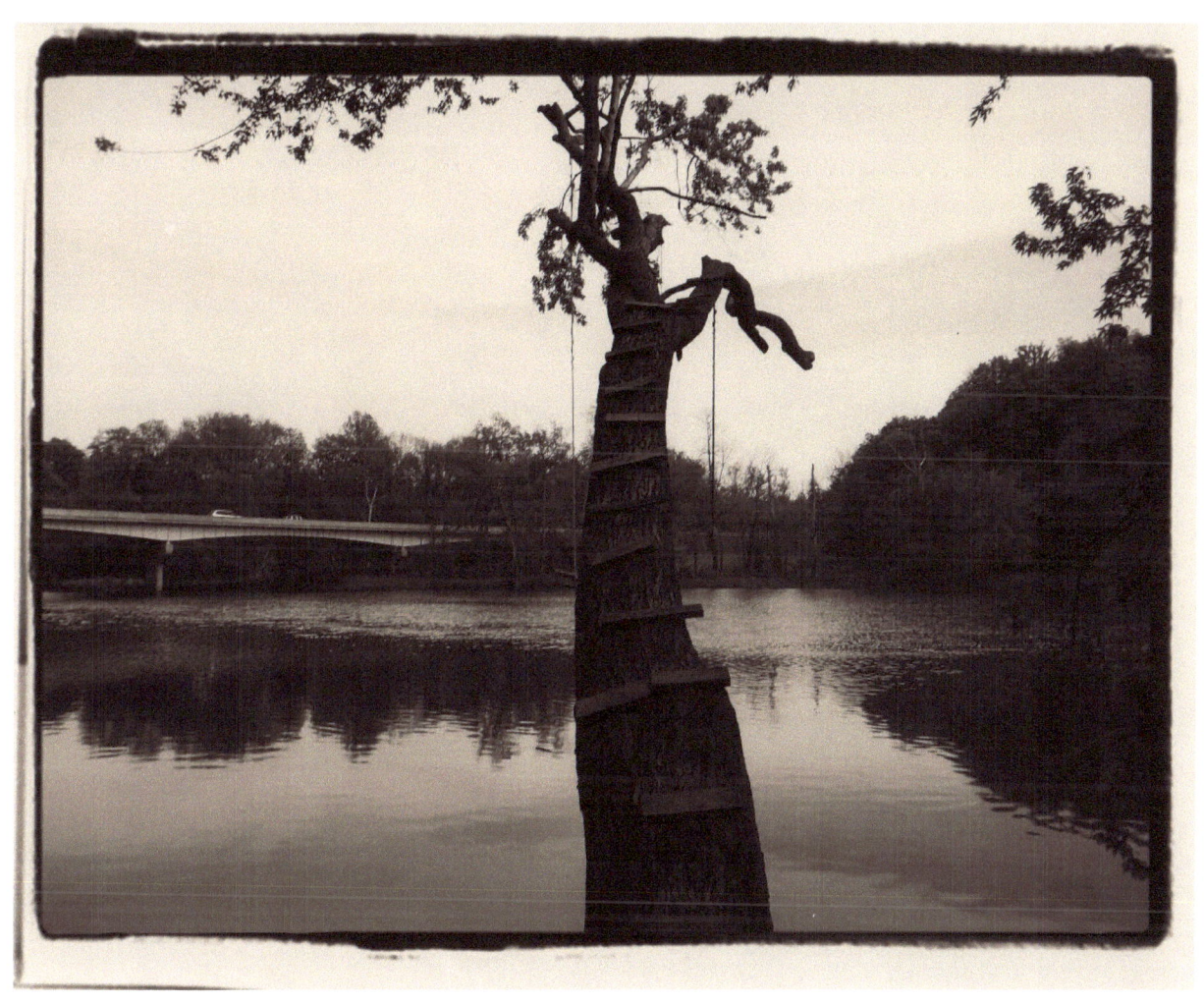

-*A place of peace, in a crazy world*-

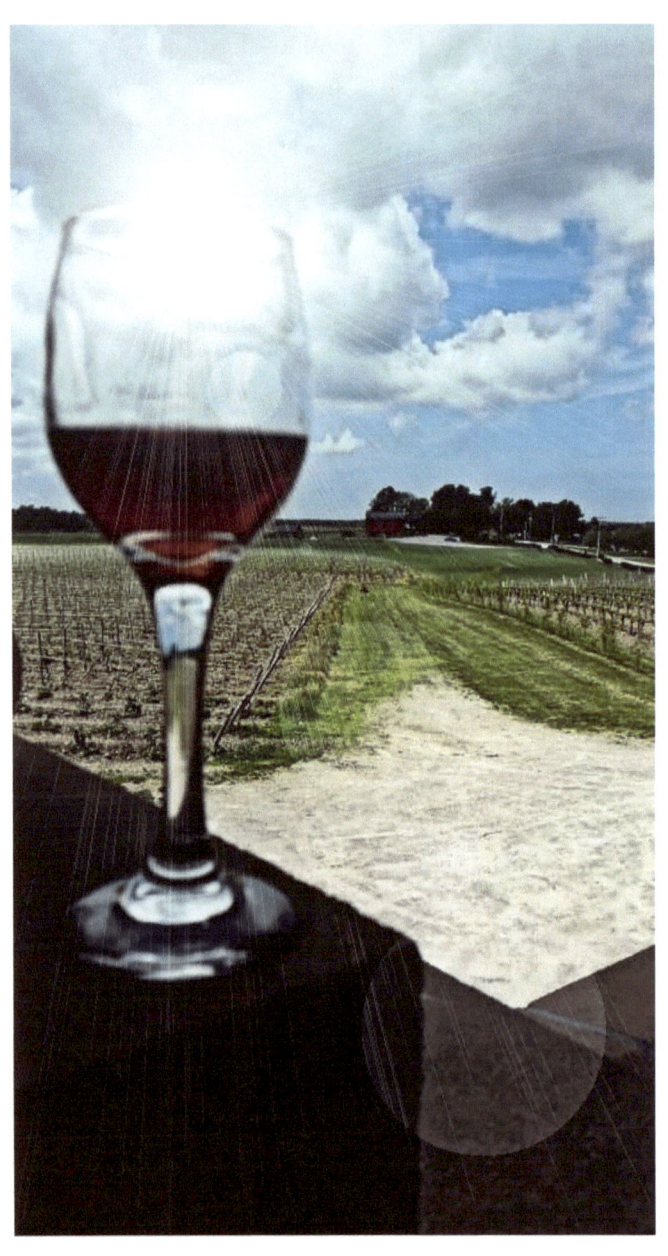

-A little wine and a little sunshine-

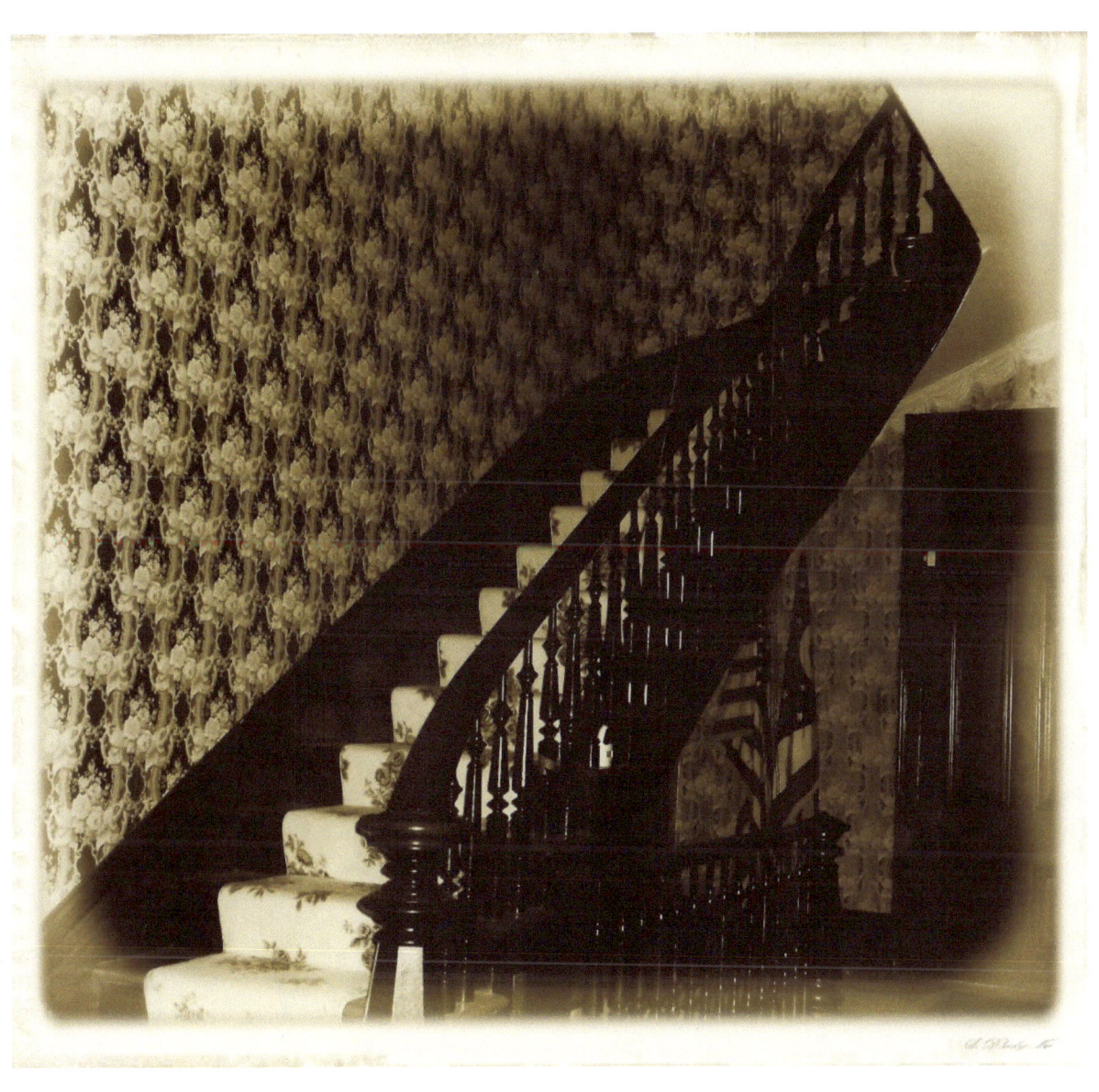

-A Stairway back in Time-

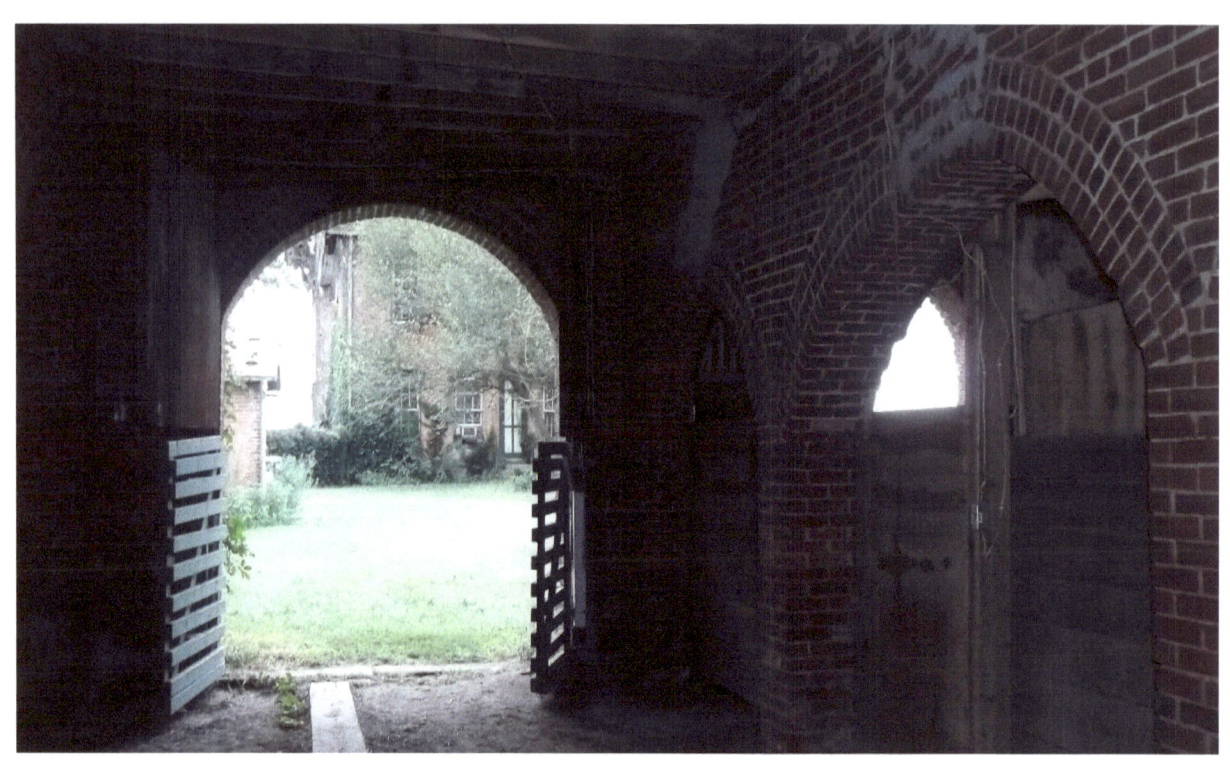

-Peaceful Barn-

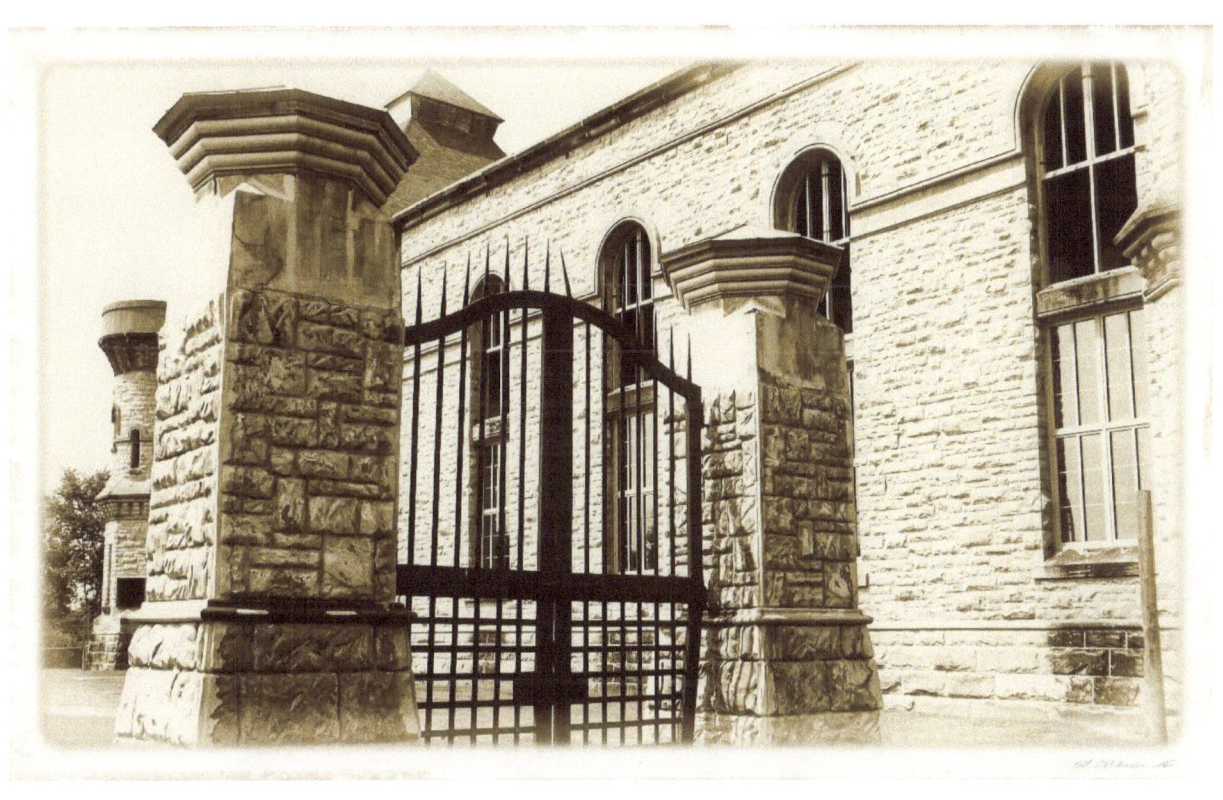

-Through the Prison Gates-

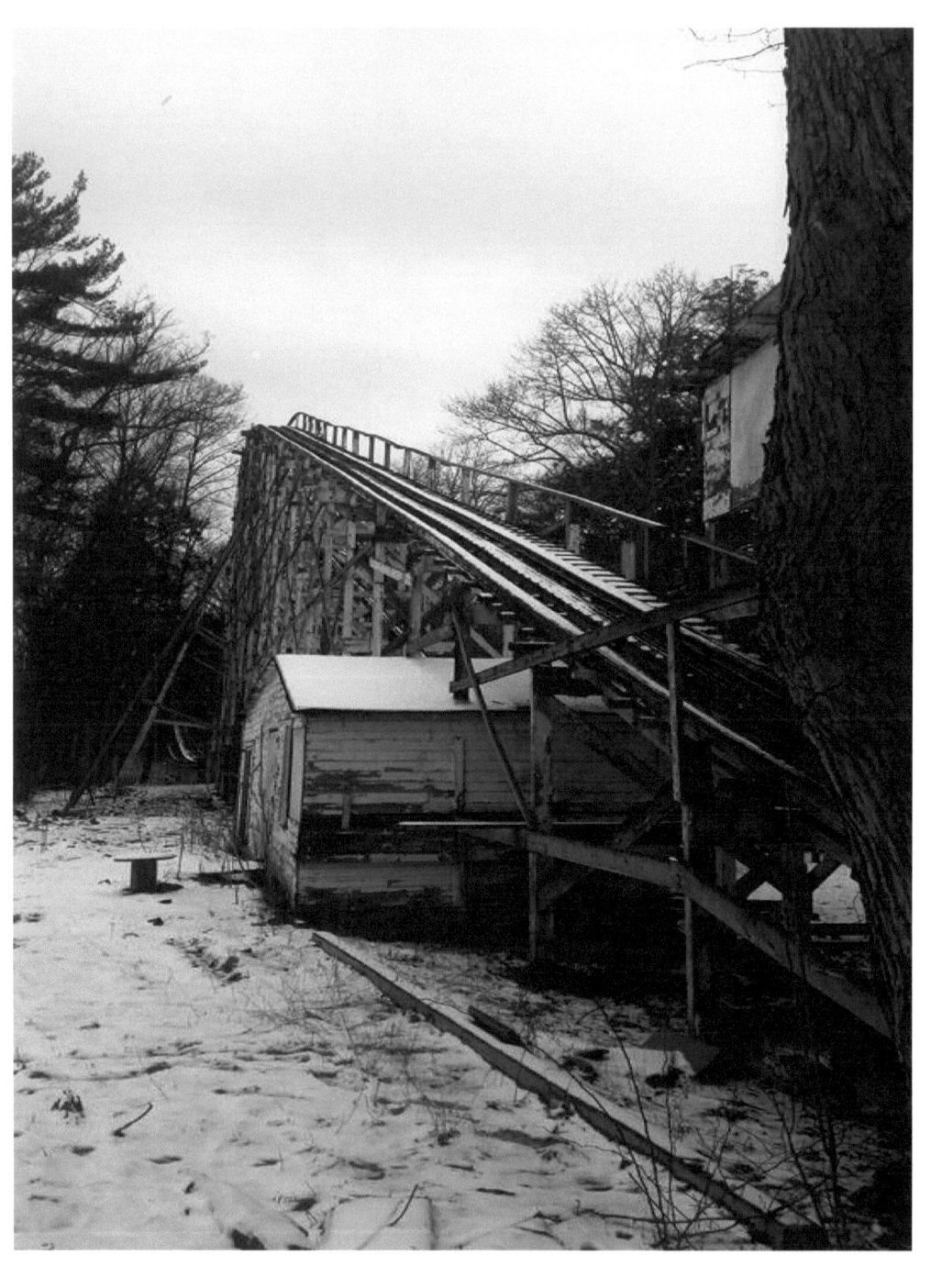

-Wintertime Walk in the Park-

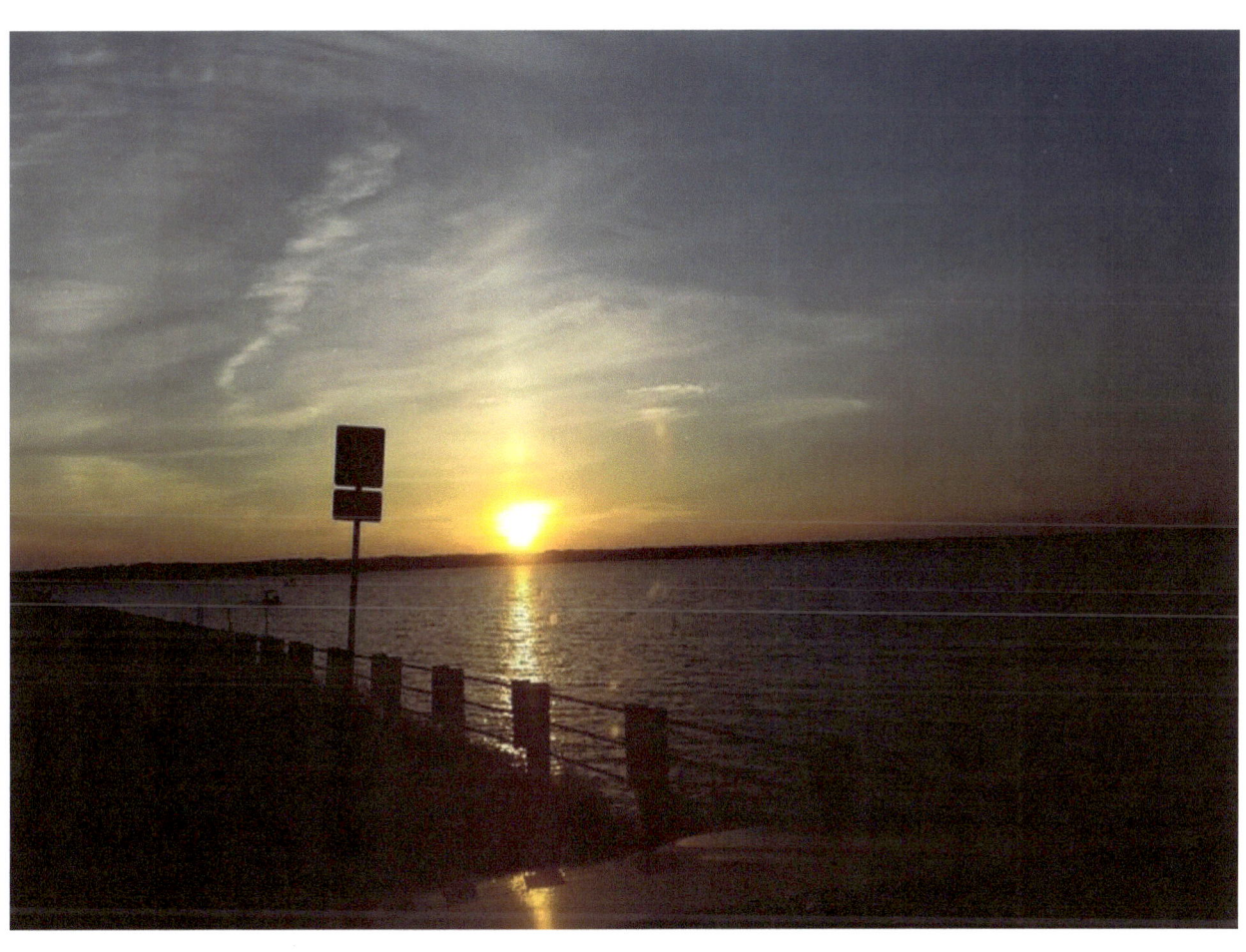

- Stunning Sunset Drive -

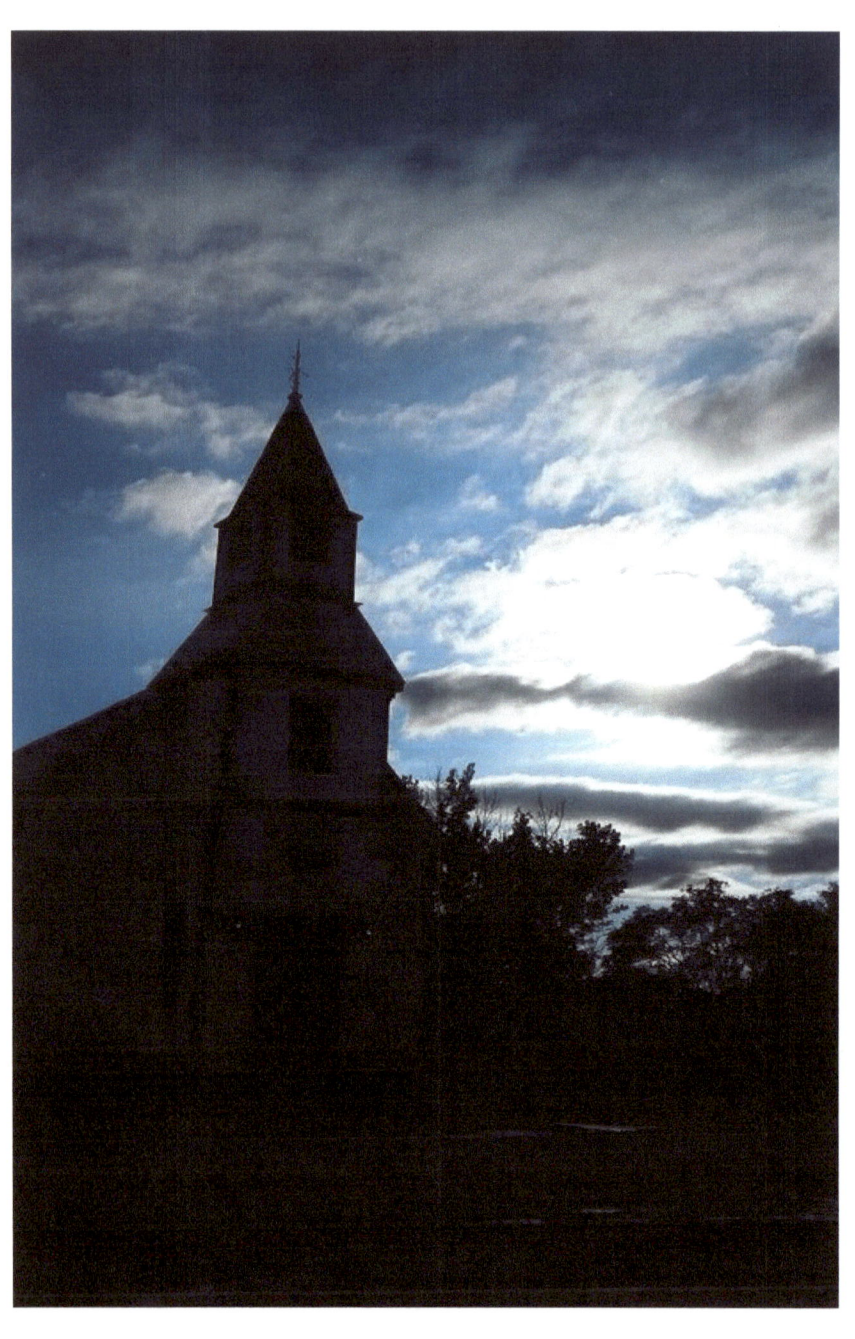

-Timeless Church-

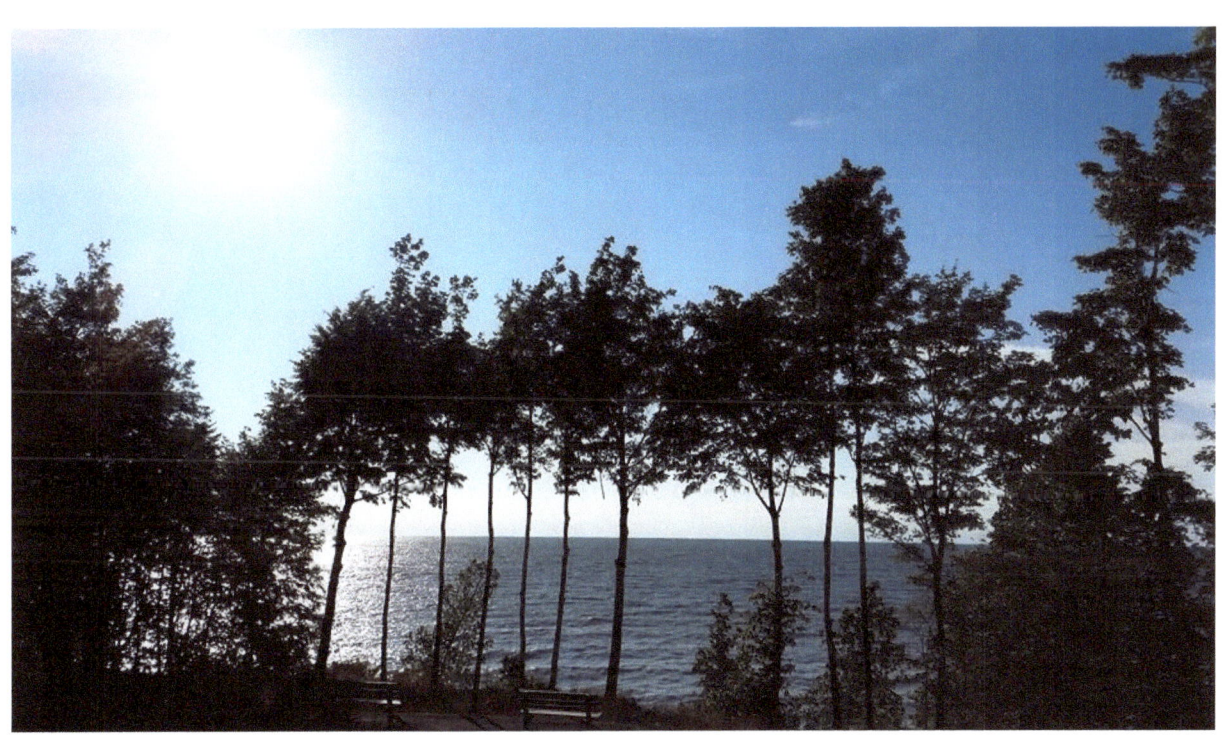

-Trees with a View-

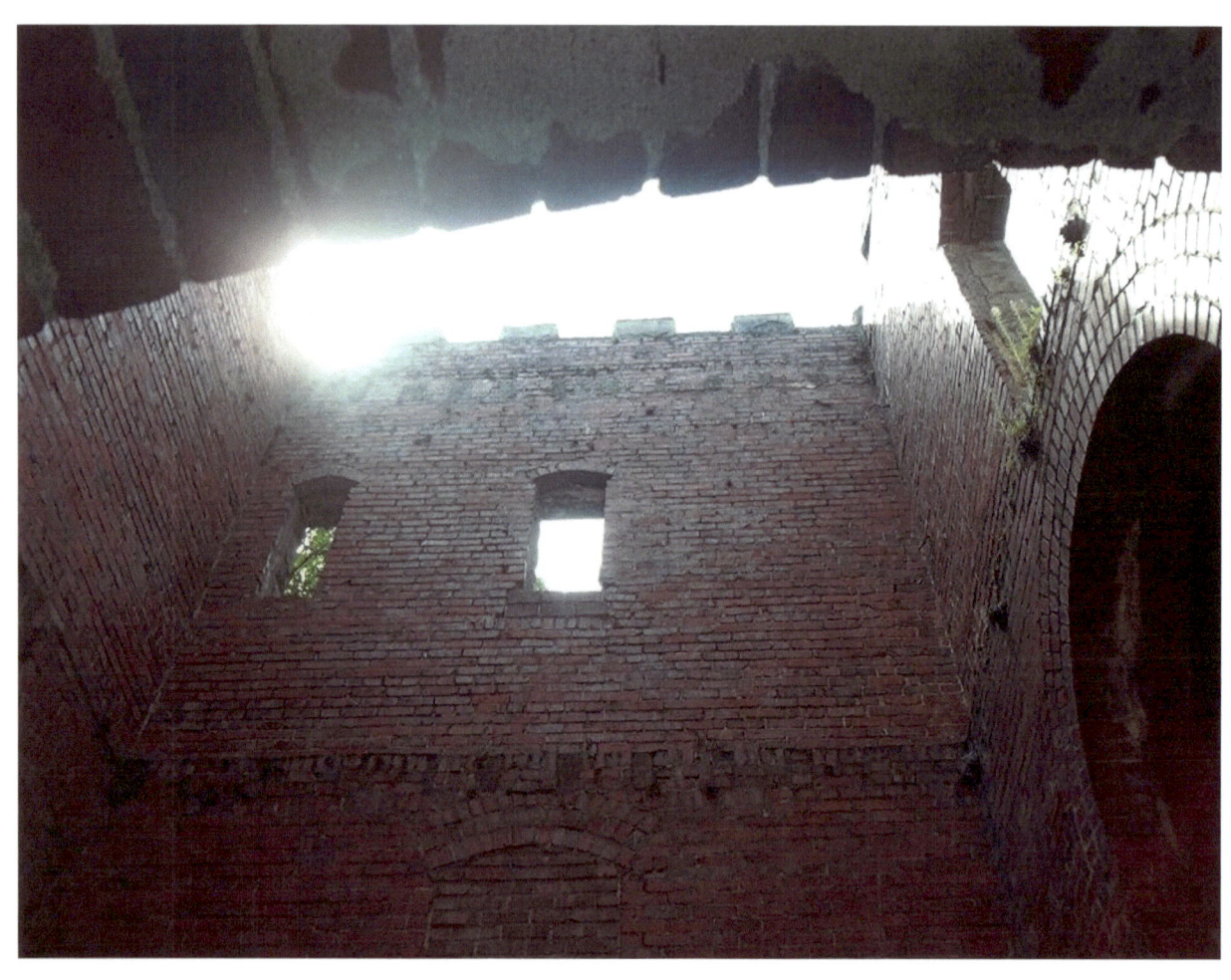

- Childhood Memories of a Castle -

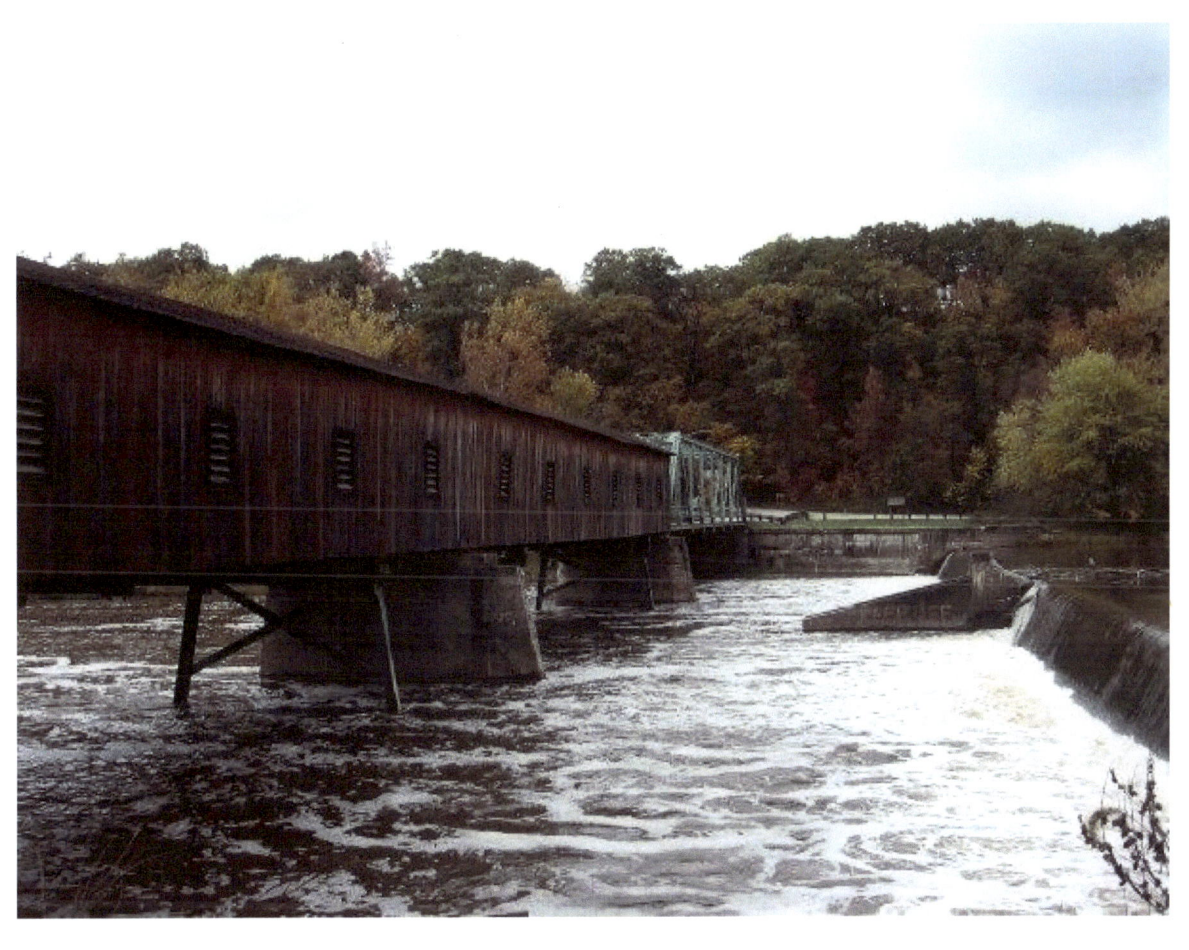

-Fall at the Bridge-

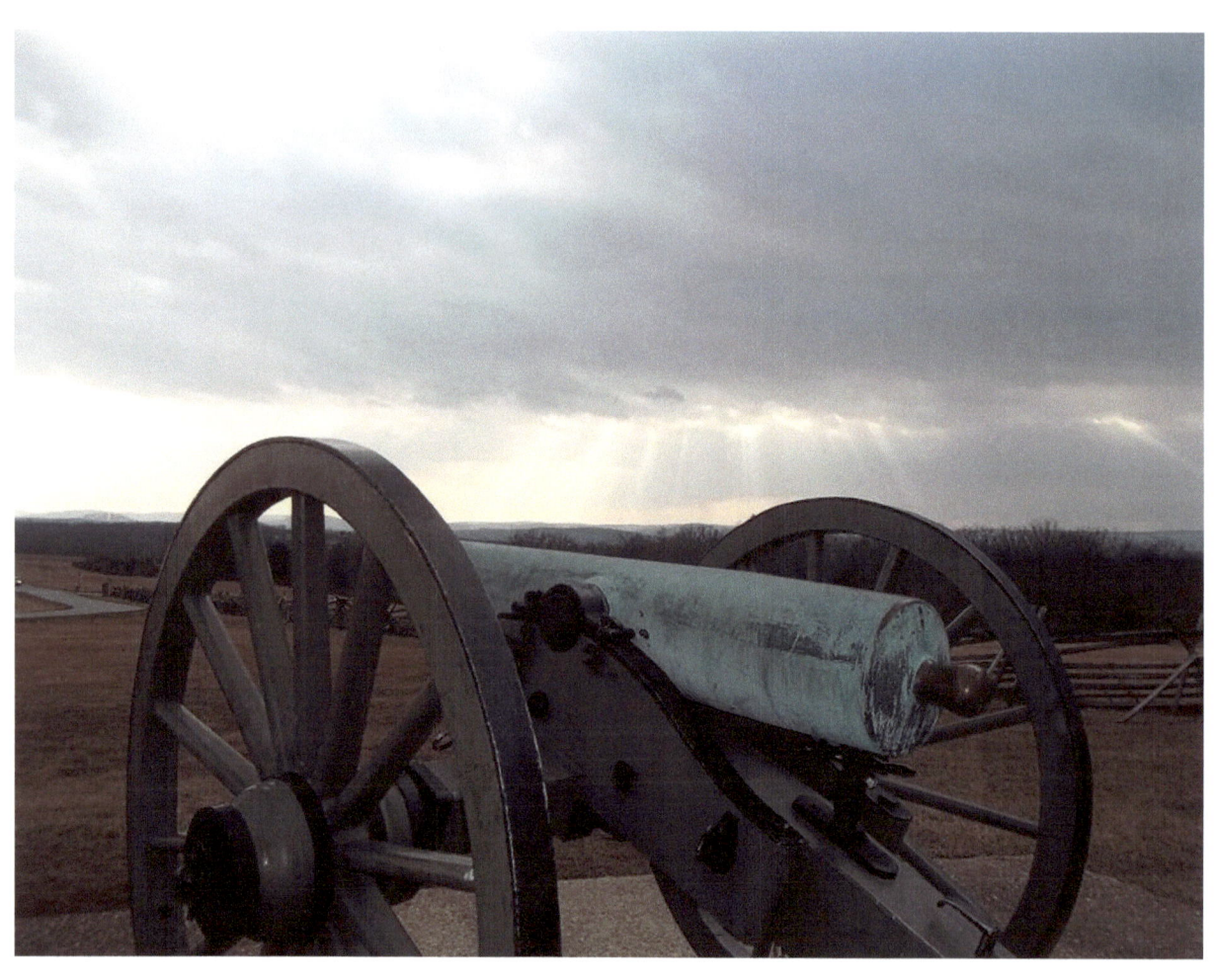

-Don't Tread on Me-

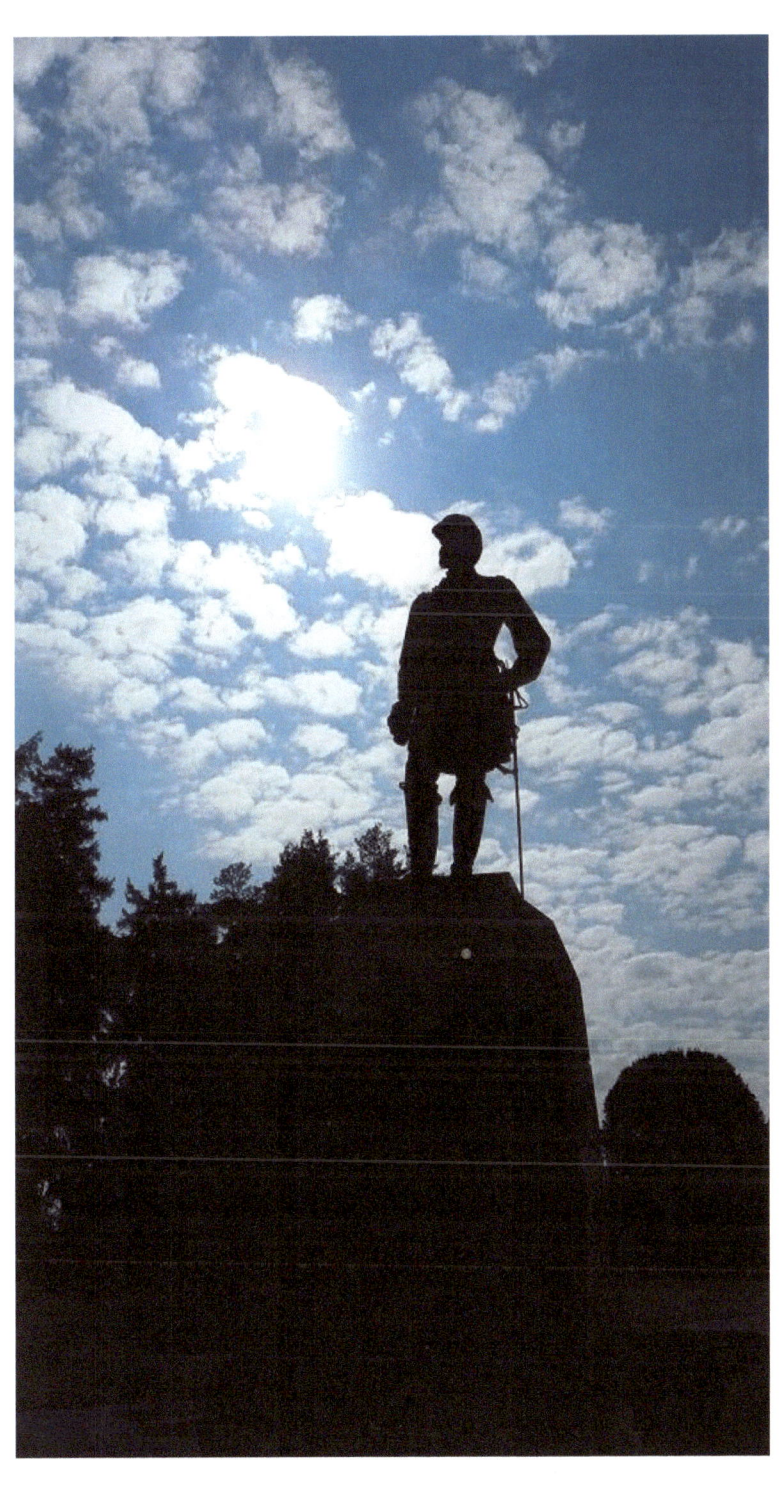

-Stand Tall, Stand Proud-

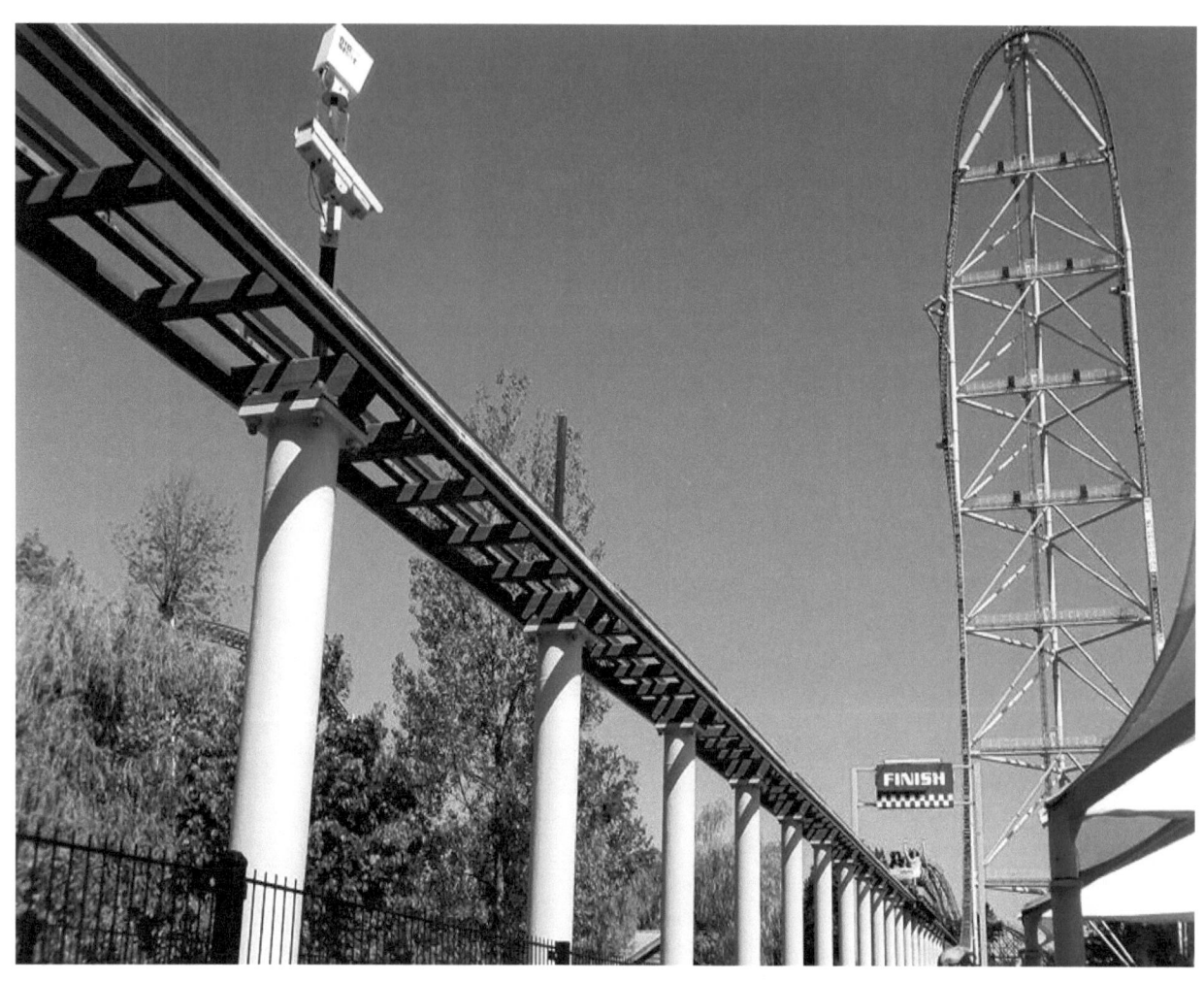

-Summertime Fun-

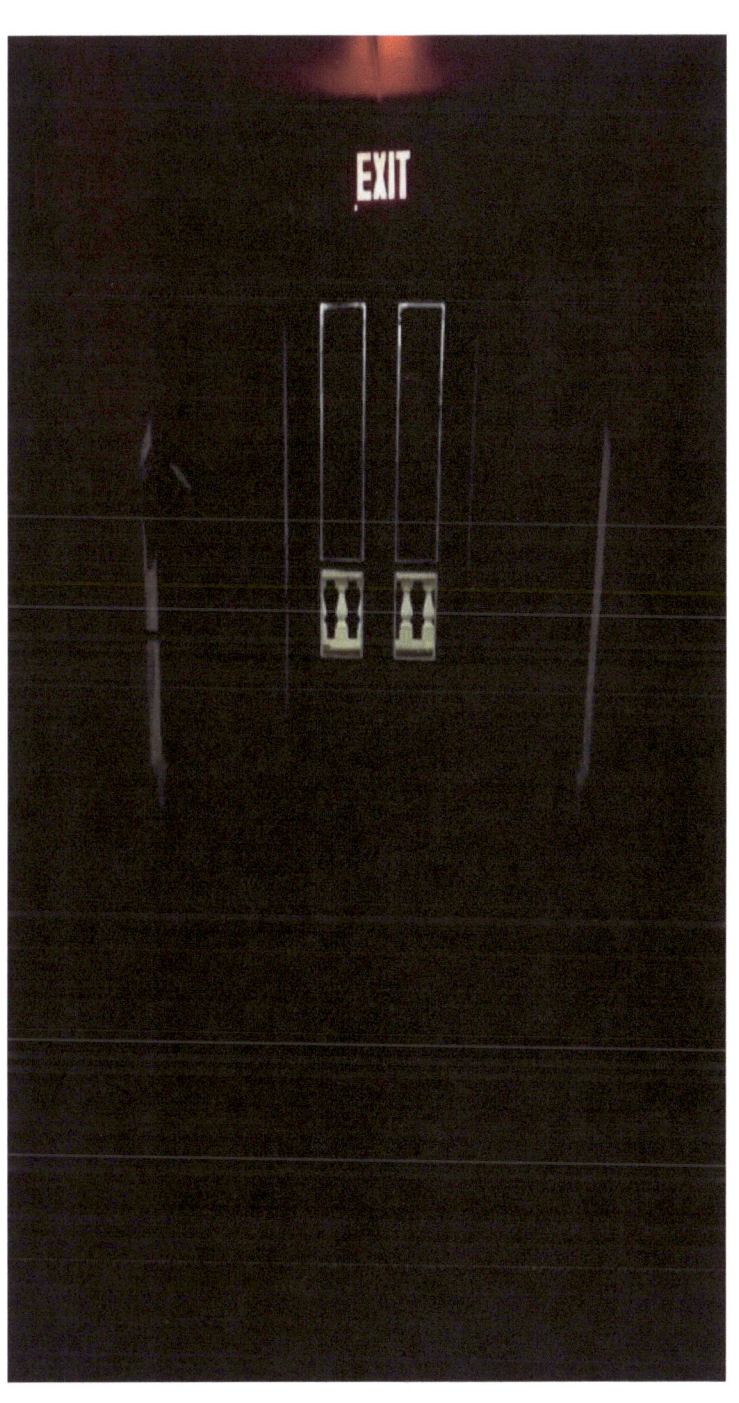

-Hallway in Time-

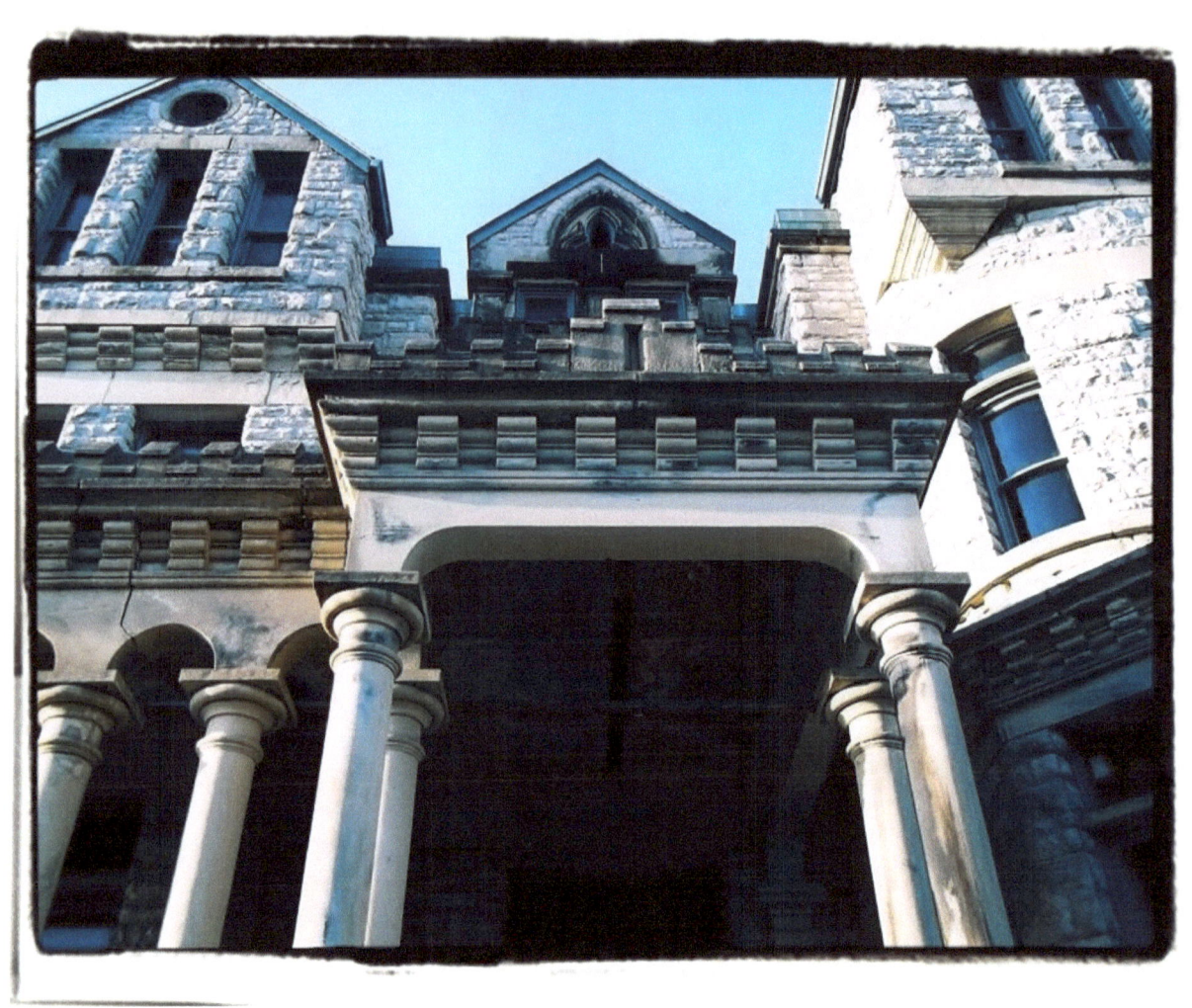

-Timeless Architecture-

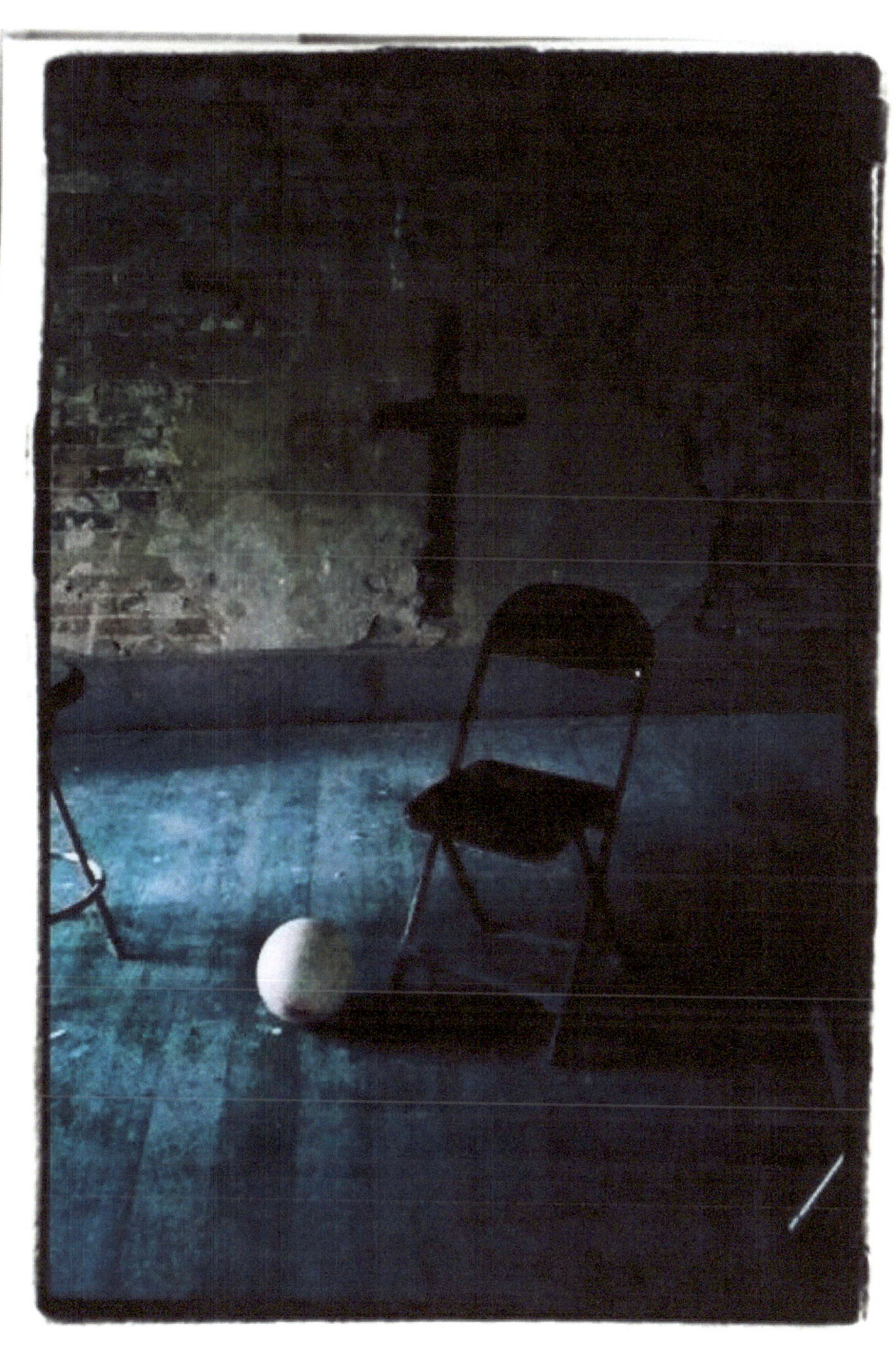

-Silent Contemplation-

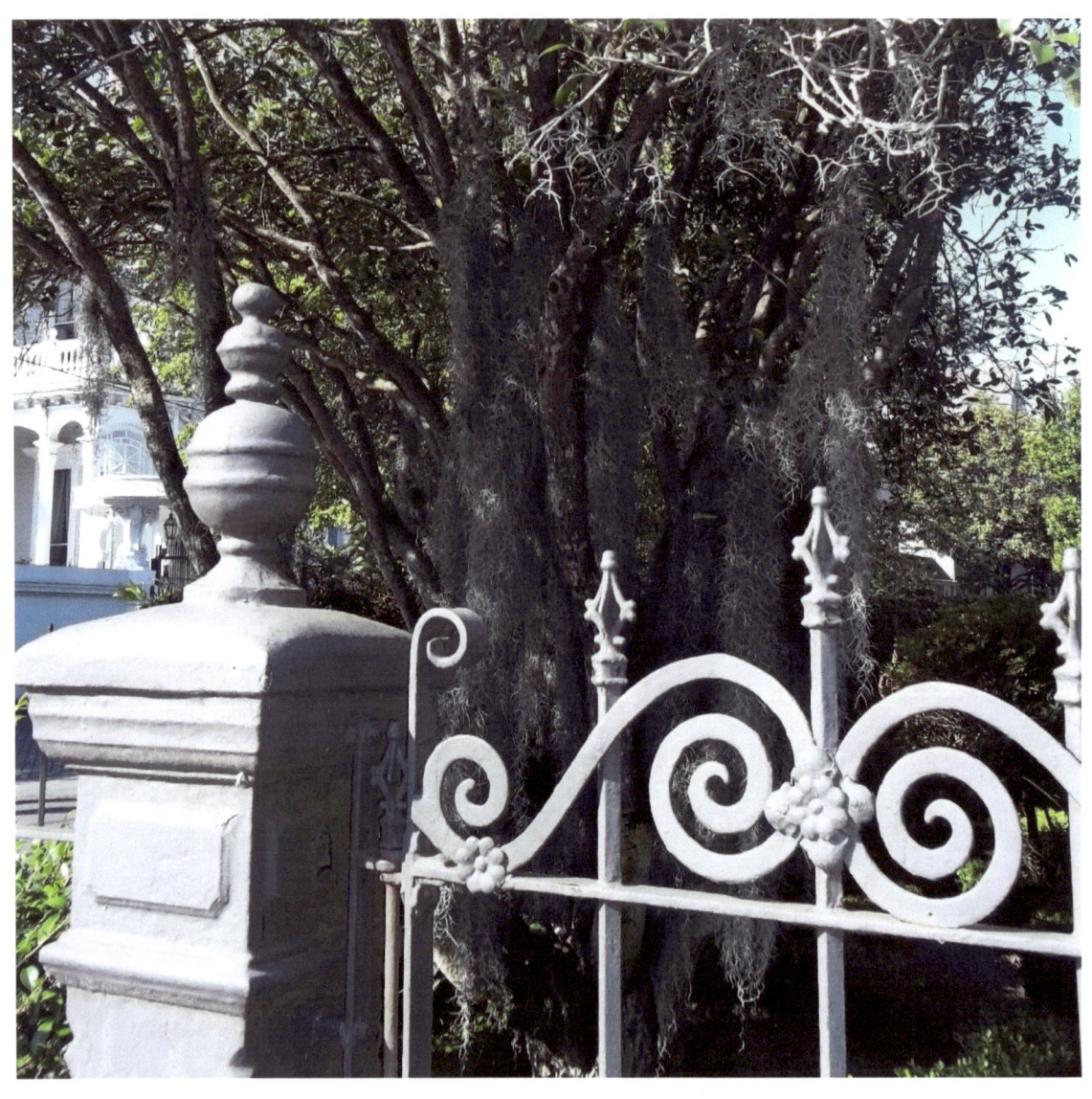

-Gateway of Beauty-

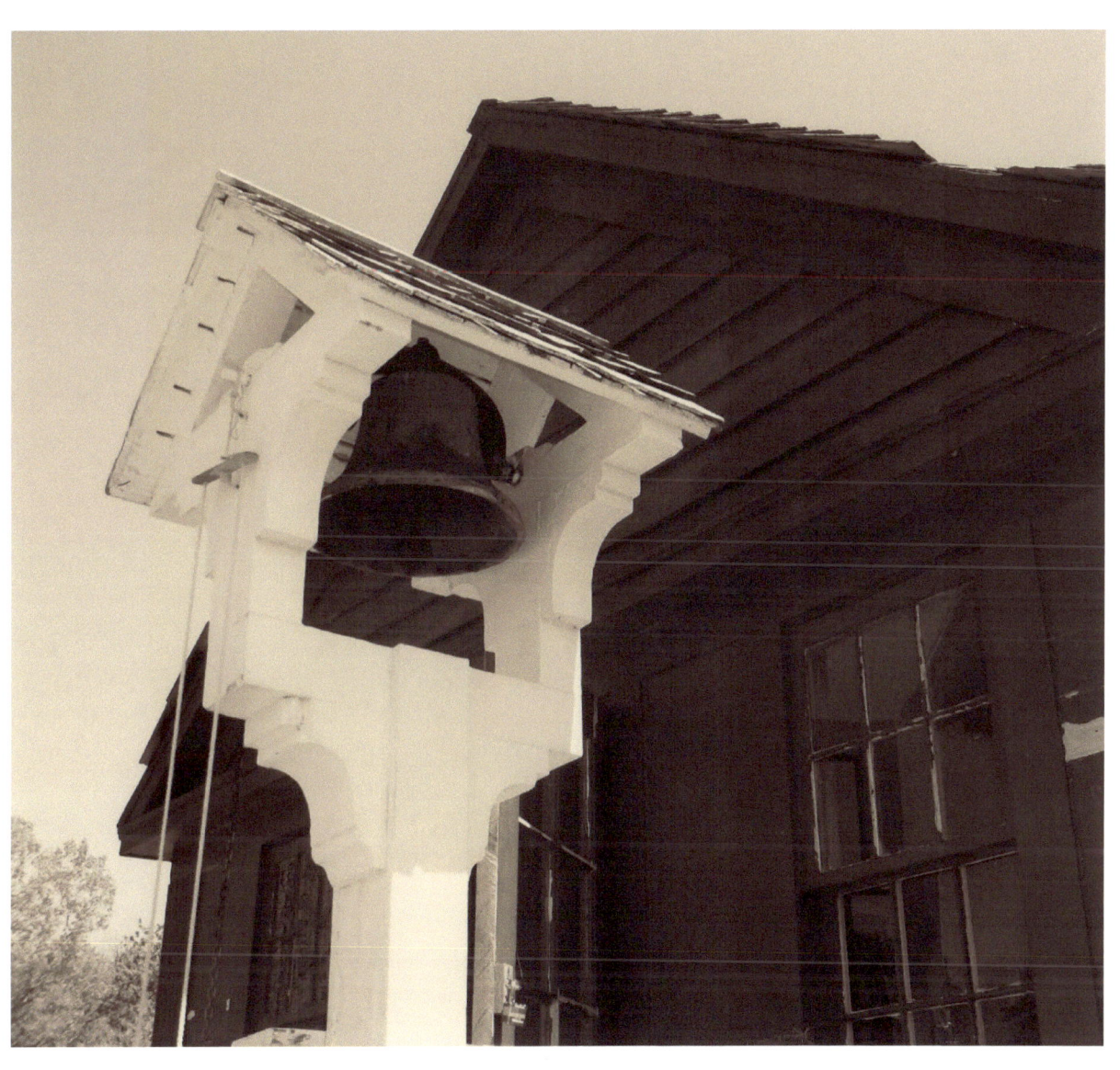

-Let the School Day Begin-

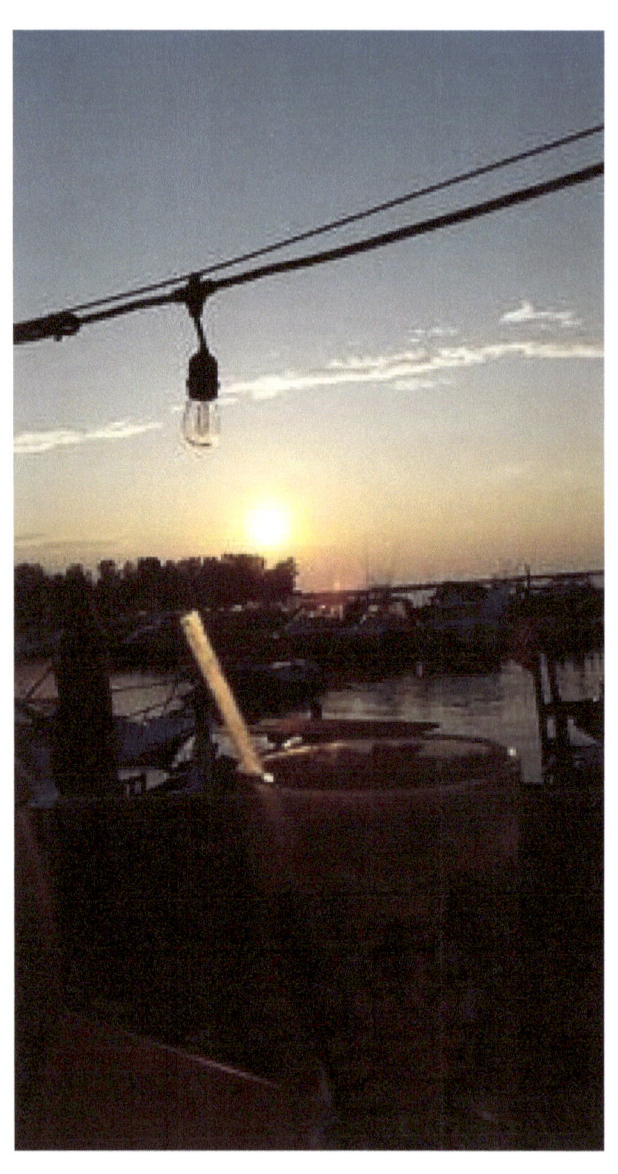

-On The Dock of the Bay-

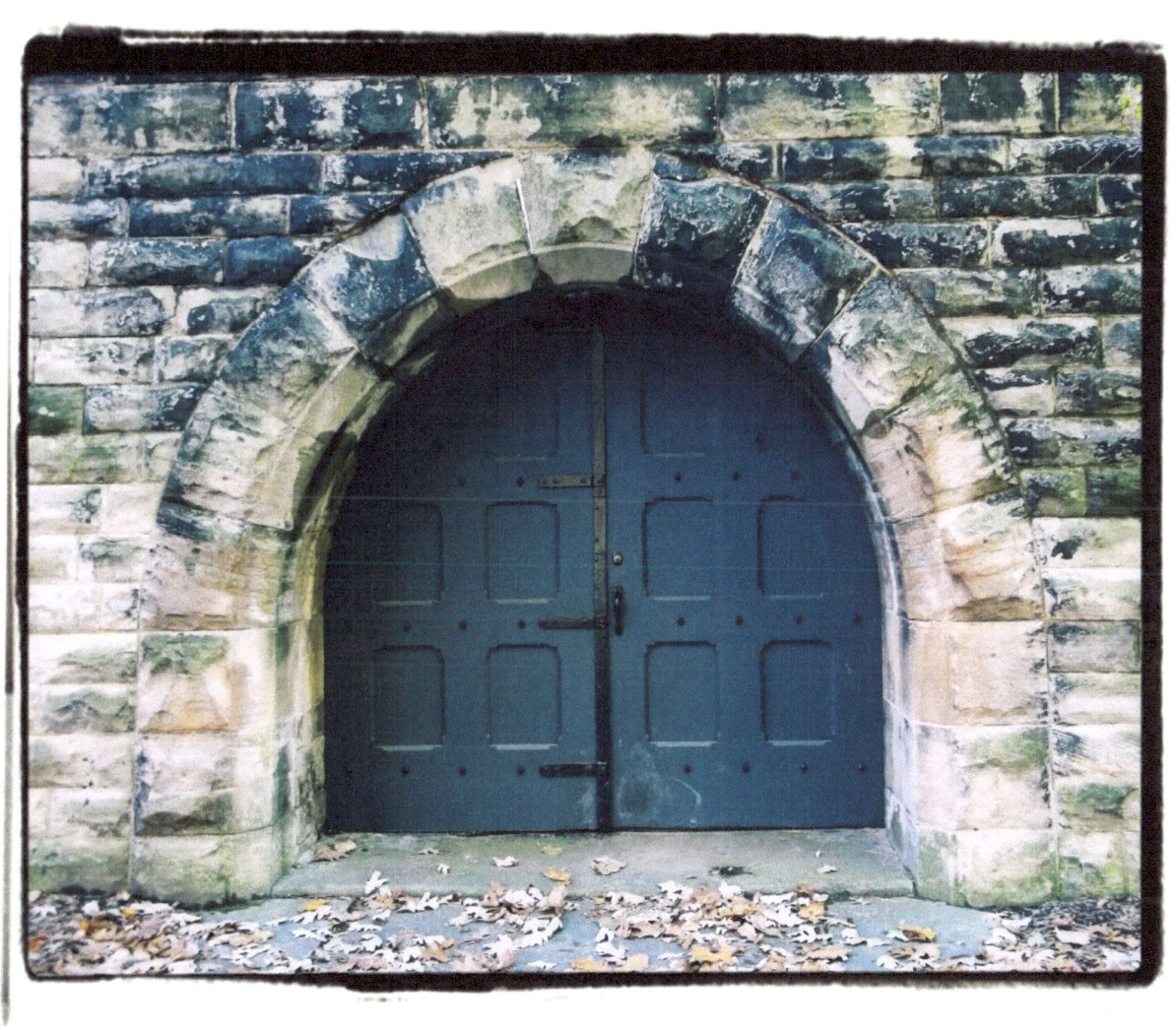

-Let Me In-

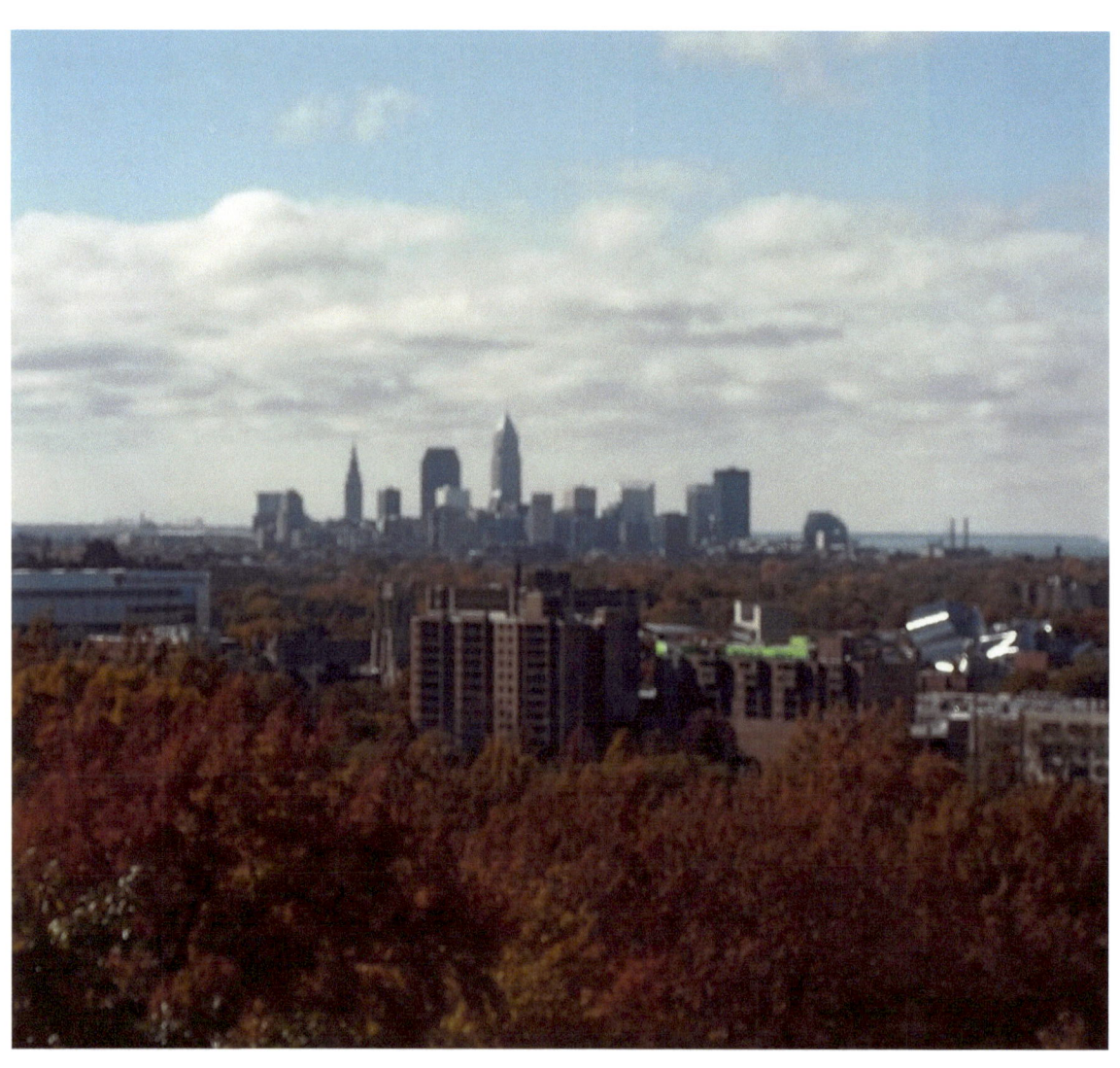

-Skyline Beauty-

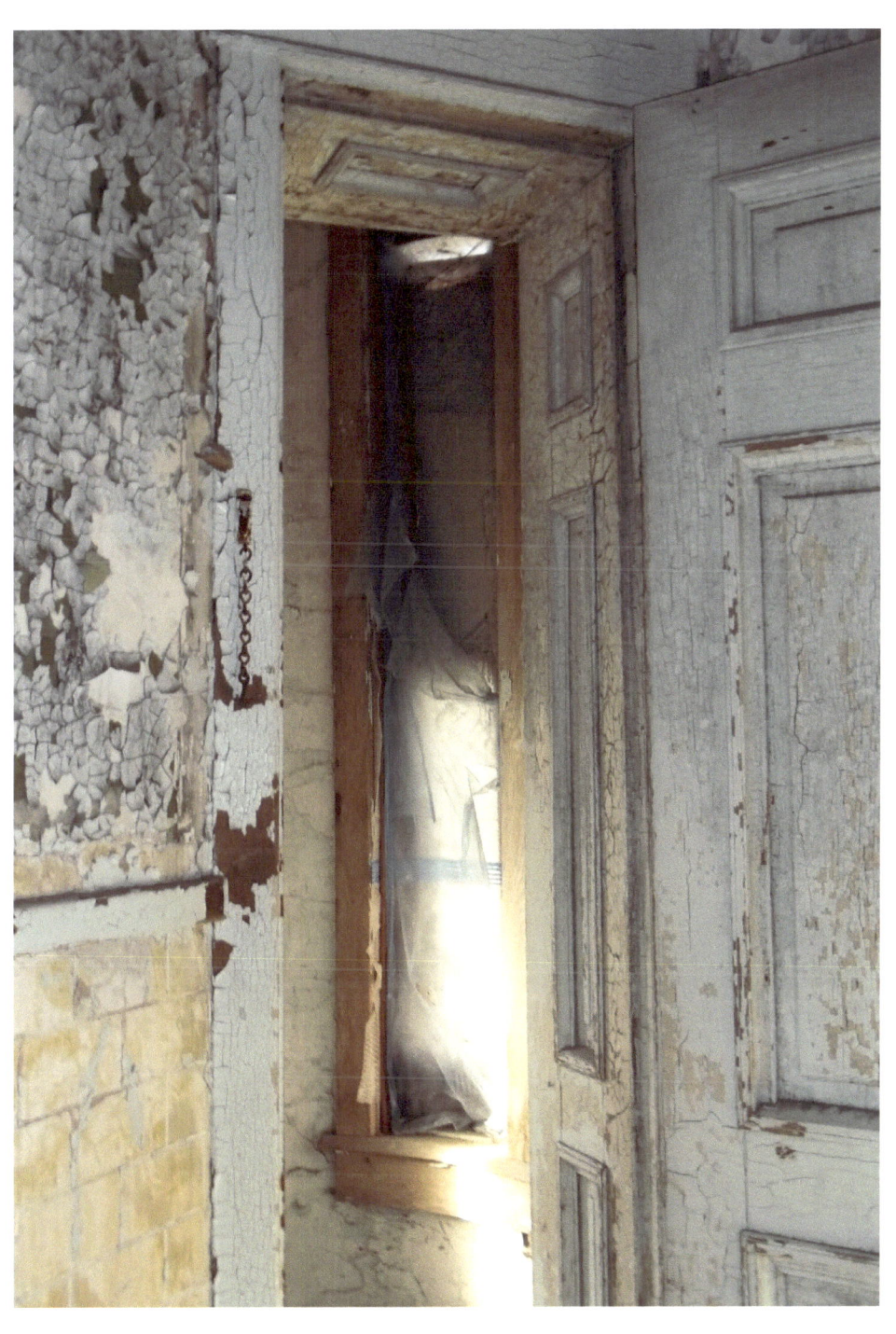

-Forgotten Doorway-

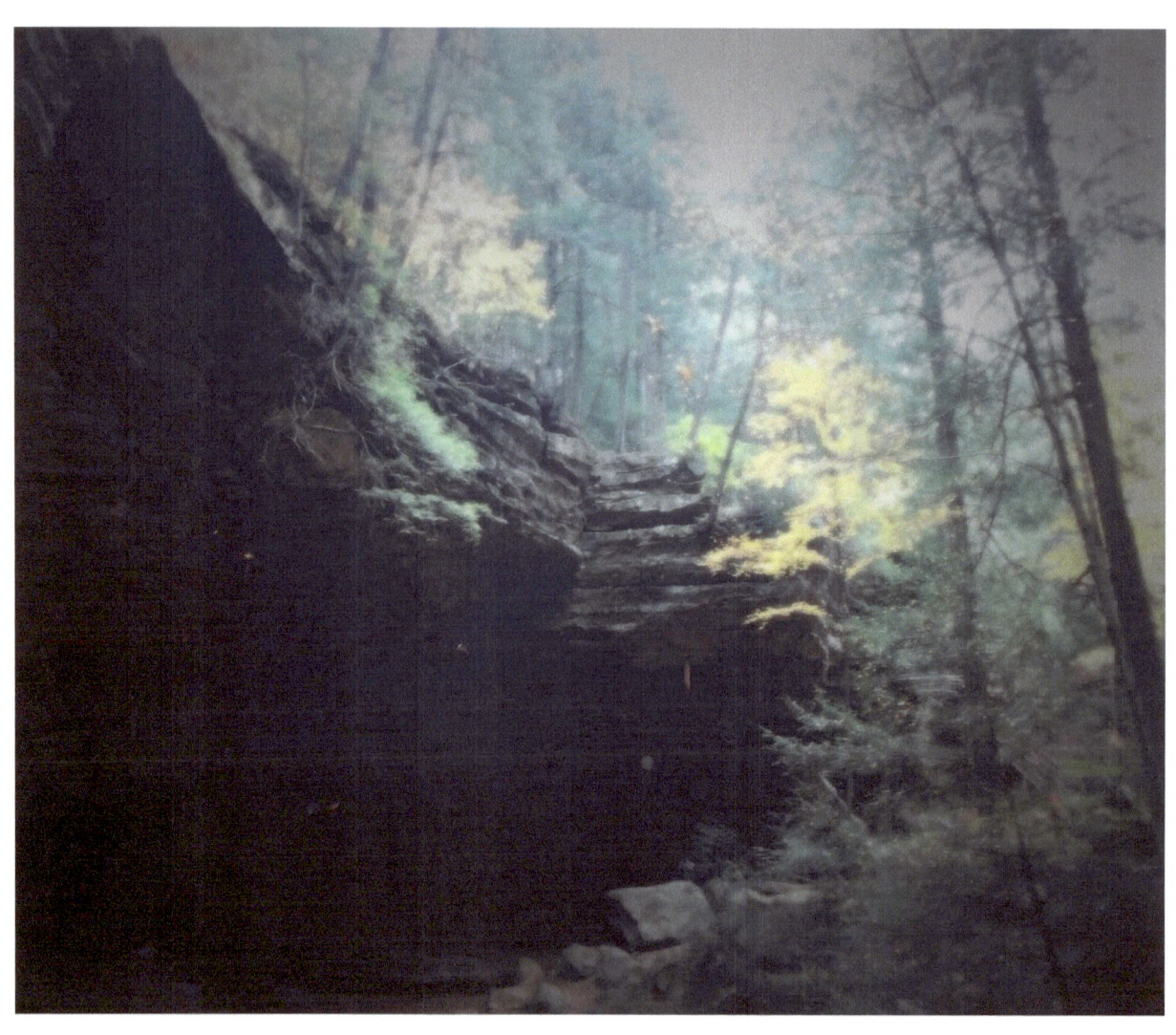

-Whispering Woods-

-Acknowledgments-

I would like to take a moment to acknowledge some of the beautiful locations in which these pictures were taken.

Shores of Lake Erie in Cleveland, Ohio

Prospect Place in Dresden, Ohio

Ohio State Reformatory

Progressive Field in Cleveland, Ohio

Geneva-on-the-Lake, Ohio

The French Quarter in New Orleans, LA

Buckner Mansion in the Garden District of New Orleans, LA

Oak Alley Plantation in Vacherie, LA

Hogback Ridge, Madison, Ohio

Soldiers & Sailors Monument, Cleveland, Ohio

Harpersfield Bridge in Ohio

South River Winery in Geneva, Ohio

Kinsman House in Warren, Ohio

Conneaut Lake Park, PA

Pymatuning Lake, PA

The Bluffs in Perry, Ohio

Squire's Castle in Willoughby Hills, Ohio

Gettysburg, PA

Cedar Point in Sandusky, Ohio

Madison Seminary in Madison, Ohio

The Lake County History Center in Ohio

Lakeview Cemetery in Cleveland, Ohio

Hocking Hills, Ohio